Lend a Hand

Exploring Service-Learning through Children's Literature

Diane Findlay

UpstartBooks

Fort Atkinson, Wisconsin

Thanks again to the wonderful public libraries that support my habit and encourage me in my projects! Special thanks again to the wonderful staff members at the Waukee and West Des Moines Public Libraries, who consistently provide service above and beyond the call of duty—may they all get big raises! Thanks again to my teacher friends who answer my odd questions and cheer me on. This book led me to many wonderful people who generously shared their experiences with service-learning in their classrooms and communities. Two who were especially and repeatedly helpful were Joe Herrity, Consultant for Community Education, Service-Learning and 21st Century Community Learning Centers for the Iowa Department of Education; and Deb Coyne, Service-Learning Coordinator for the North Adams School District in Massachusetts. I am grateful to you all.

Published by UpstartBooks
W5527 Highway 106
P.O. Box 800
Fort Atkinson, Wisconsin 53538-0800
1-800-448-4887

Contents

Introduction

While researching and writing an earlier book, *Characters with Character: Using Children's Literature in Character Education,* I was struck by how often two concepts emerged as fundamental to developing character: 1) a gut-level awareness that other people are as important and valuable as you are, and 2) the ability and desire to empathize, or at least sympathize, with others. So I was delighted to have a chance to further explore and promote those concepts through this book about service-learning, which seems to be the epitome of a win-win proposition. While pursuing clear academic curricular goals, students develop respect for others, empathy, self-knowledge, self-esteem, practical life skills and good citizenship habits through engaging in real community service projects.

The idea of service-learning, as a strategy distinct from community service volunteering, has been developing and gaining support around the nation over the past 30 years or so. A recent report from the National Commission on Service-Learning indicates that, as of 1999, nearly one third of the nation's public schools included service-learning activities as part of their curriculum. While that is an impressive statistic, many of those schools' service-learning opportunities involved only one or a few teachers. High schools were more likely than elementary schools to use service-learning strategies, and most public school students still did not have an opportunity to experience this powerful mode of learning.

What exactly is service-learning? Here are some representative definitions:

- "Service-learning is a method of teaching and learning which engages students in solving problems and addressing issues in their school or greater community as part of the academic curriculum." (Iowa Department of Education)

- "Service-learning is a powerful strategy for teaching and learning, which allows young people to deepen and demonstrate their learning and at the same time develop a strong sense of civic responsibility." (John Glenn, Chair, The National Commission on Service-Learning)

- "A service-learning program provides ... a student with opportunities to use newly-acquired skills and knowledge in real-life situations in their own communities...." (The Commission on National and Community Service, now the Corporation for National and Community Service)

- "Service-learning ... provides a compelling answer to the perennial question: 'Why do I need to learn this stuff?'" (General Colin Powell, founding chairman of America's Promise)

- "Service-learning helps translate book lessons into life lessons." (Representative Pete Hoekstra, member of Congress)

Where service-learning initiatives have taken place, response from students, teachers and representatives of the served communities is enthusiastic. In fact, service-learning has attracted so much positive press that during the 1990s Congress passed several initiatives that provided support and funding for local service-learning programs. And the National Commission on Service-Learning, in its 2001 report titled "Learning in Deed: The Power of Service-Learning for American Schools," issued this challenge: "Every child in an

American primary and secondary school should participate in quality service-learning every year as an integral and essential part of his or her education experience."

This book explores, in eight chapters, social issues or arenas of activity in which elementary school students might get involved through service-learning initiatives. It might be used as a starting point for schools or teachers wanting to experiment with service-learning or to support and enrich ongoing service-learning activities. Each chapter provides an introduction to the issue or arena of activity; an annotated list of fiction, nonfiction and nonprint titles exploring the subject; examples of related service-learning projects; and ideas for how to identify and act on needs in your local community in a service-learning mode. The goal is to help you guide students through four steps related to each issue: 1) Understanding the issue in general (What's it all about?), 2) Making an emotional connection (Why should we care?), 3) Identifying needs in the local community (What problems do we face right here?) and 4) Taking action (What can we do about it?) in ways that tie directly to curriculum goals and standards.

The titles represent the best I could find in classic and contemporary children's literature. Some are award winners, some were positively reviewed or highly recommended, some are classics that have stood the test of time and some are simply favorites of mine. I encourage you to add your own favorites and to adapt the ideas and activities to your choice of literature, your particular curriculum standards and the needs of your class and your community. All listed titles were in print or readily available in libraries at press time.

I'd like to recommend some specific resources that may assist in your efforts to provide service-learning opportunities in the classroom. The first is a pair of books by Barbara A. Lewis that are packed full of specific ideas, examples, contact resources and how-to lists related to their respective titles, *The Kid's Guide to Service Projects* and *The Kid's Guide to Social Action*. Both are from Free Spirit Publishing. A series of books on service-learning, written as easy reading for grades 3–5 and published by Children's Press, might be useful as a source of ideas for individual students motivated to go beyond classroom projects. Titles include *Volunteering to Help with Animals, Volunteering to Help Seniors, Volunteering to Help in Your Neighborhood* and others. Three Web sites offer excellent introductions and resources related to service-learning in general. They are Seanet, the State Education Agency site (www.seanetonline.org), the National Youth Leadership Council's site (www.nylc.org) and the National Service-Learning Clearinghouse site (www.servicelearning.org). SERVEnet (www.servenet.org) provides information, accessed by zip code and other search criteria, about volunteer service activities and organizations needing help in your local area. Finally, the Common Cents New York site (www.commoncents.org) is full of exciting and inspiring information about this New York City organization that started as a neighborhood "penny harvest" to help the homeless and blossomed into a full-spectrum service-learning organization offering curriculum materials and working with 940 local schools. Their projects and support materials address several of the issues covered in this book.

Best of luck with your service-learning adventures!

Hunger and the Homeless

Nearly every American community, from small towns to huge cities, includes residents who are hungry or homeless. In earlier days homeless people were sometimes referred to as "bums," "vagrants," "bag ladies" or "tramps." Most were men, and the general public consensus was that they were lazy or crazy and should pull themselves together and get jobs. We live in what we hope are more enlightened times, in one of the wealthiest nations in the world. Yet while most of us live comfortably, even extravagantly by global standards, too many of America's poor are hungry and homeless through no fault of their own. Many are people "just like us" (and the children in our classrooms), who have lost their jobs or suffered other economic setbacks and who, like us, try hard to build better lives for themselves and their families. They try to survive and keep their pride and dignity as best they can. We use gentler, less judgmental terms now to describe our "homeless" or "street people," yet the problem grows alarmingly. With major cutbacks in government funding for a host of social programs, and a rising cost of living, we have more people living in poverty, more homeless and hungry, each year. And more women, children and whole families are hungry and homeless than in the past. While many individuals; local, state and federal agencies; and profit and nonprofit organizations do what they can to provide for the needs of the hungry and the homeless, these needs grow and the cost in human suffering and lost human potential is staggering.

Who are the hungry or the homeless in your community, and how can you help them? Here are some topics to explore within the theme of hunger and homelessness.

- ♥ Causes of homelessness.

- ♥ Realities of homelessness in your community—where do homeless people sleep and what do they eat?

- ♥ Sources of information about hunger and homelessness in your community.

- ♥ Services and facilities for the hungry and homeless in your community.

- ♥ Seeing the hungry and homeless as "real people."

- ♥ Helping the hungry and homeless maintain or recover their pride and dignity.

Resources on Hunger and the Homeless

Use these resources to increase understanding and to put a human face on the problems of hunger and homelessness.

Fiction

♥ ***Anna Casey's Place in the World*** by Adrian Fogelin. Peachtree Publishers, Ltd., 2001. 3–5. This gentle, engaging novel features a 12-year-old orphan who has run out of relatives and entered foster care. She longs for a permanent family and begins to feel at home among an appealing and believable cast of characters that includes a prickly foster brother, a homeless Vietnam veteran, a gaggle of neighborhood kids and an eccentric biology teacher. When her worst fears of losing her home seem about to come true, Anna finds her "place in the world" right under her nose.

♥ ***Darnell Rock Reporting*** by Walter Dean Myers. Bantam Doubleday Dell, 1996. 3–5. Thirteen-year-old Darnell is not a bad kid, but he's not interested in school and tends to get into trouble. When the principal warns him it's time to do something positive or face the consequences, he volunteers for the school newspaper. Almost accidentally, he becomes an advocate for a homeless man and discovers that his words can make a difference.

♥ ***Dew Drop Dead*** by James Howe. Simon & Schuster, 1999. 3–5. Two parallel plots converge as 13-year-old Sebastian and his pals Corrie and David investigate a murder at an abandoned inn and help establish a homeless shelter in a church basement.

♥ ***Holes*** by Louis Sachar. Random House, 2000. 5+. Newbery Medal Book, ALA Notable Children's Book. When Stanley Yelnats is unjustly sent to a sinister boy's correctional facility, he blames his bad luck on a curse placed on his "no-good-dirty-rotten-pig-stealing great great grandfather." At the facility, Stanley encounters an evil, tormenting staff; an obsessed, cruel warden; the first real friends he's ever made; and a mystery. As Stanley suffers the realities of Camp Green Lake, he stumbles upon his destiny and creates a ripple of hope and redemption for a whole cast of ne'er-do-well characters. This multiple award winner is darkly humorous, shockingly brutal in parts and downright creepy, but irresistible and thought provoking for mature students.

♥ ***The Homeless Hibernating Bear*** by Kids Livin' Life. Gold Leaf Press, 1993. K–5. Written by "homeless, post-homeless and low-income children," this picture book tells a story of homeless children rescuing a bear cub that is lost in Salt Lake City. Through the book, its young creators "tell their own story of homelessness in their own way." Not polished or literary but touching and effective, this book shows disadvantaged kids taking creative, powerful action to address their circumstances.

♥ ***I Can Hear the Sun*** by Patricia Polacco. Penguin Putnam, 1999. 2–5. Fondo lives at the home for unwanted children, but spends his time with Stephanie Michele at the nearby science center and bird sanctuary. He befriends the homeless regulars in the park and bonds with a blind goose. Fondo believes that the geese talk to him, that he can hear the sun and that someday he will fly away to a happier life. When the home labels him "special needs" and plans to send him away, it's time to test his plan and see how far faith and hope will take him.

♥ ***The King of Dragons*** by Carol Fenner. Aladdin Paperbacks, 2000. 4–5. Homeless 11-year-old Ian and his Vietnam War veteran father have taken up residence in an abandoned courthouse. When his father disappears and the courthouse comes alive with renovations to house a museum kite exhibit, Ian is torn between his fear of being discovered and his fascination with the people and the process going on under his hidden, watchful eyes. A wonderful story of loneliness, fear, wishes, magic, learning and hope.

♥ ***The Lady in the Box*** by Ann McGovern. Turtle Books, 1997. K–3. Lizzie and Ben find an old woman living in a cardboard box in their neighborhood. They bring her food, though they aren't supposed to talk to strangers. They are distressed when a shop owner forces the woman to leave the warm grate in front of his store and move on, so they decide to tell their mother, after all. Her caring response helps the children learn that even small efforts can make a difference.

♥ *Monkey Island* by Paula Fox. Bantam Doubleday Dell, 1993. 3–5. Eleven-year-old Clay has more worries than any child should. His father disappeared, he and his mother live in a horrible welfare hotel and now she's gone, too. Clay takes to the streets and forms a sort of family with two homeless men. When pneumonia lands him in the hospital, social services catches up with him and eventually reunites him with his mother. The weight of Clay's bitter experience coexists with hope for a fresh start. This sobering, believable account offers insight into the many different faces and stories that make up America's homeless population.

♥ *Sammy Keyes and the Sisters of Mercy* by Wendelin Van Draanen. Knopf, 1999. 4–7. Smart-mouthed, irreverent Sammy, whom students may know from other Sammy Keyes mysteries, is serving junior high detention time by helping at St. Mary's Church. When valuables begin to disappear Sammy becomes first a suspect and then self-appointed sleuth intent on solving the mystery. Lively characters and lots of action weave together parallel plots involving the church robberies, a homeless girl, a traveling troupe of singing nuns and lots of softball action.

♥ *Someplace to Go* by Maria Testa. Albert Whitman & Company, 1996. 2–5. In this fictional first-person account, Davey describes going to school and keeping himself safe and out of trouble while his mother works and his brother looks for work. The three meet each evening at the shelter where they are staying until they can get back on their feet. While the tone is warm and the story simply told, it doesn't shy away from the dangers and distress of homelessness and hunger.

♥ *Sophie and the Sidewalk Man* by Stephanie S. Tolan. Simon & Schuster, 1992. 2–5. Eight-year-old Sophie is desperate to buy the one-of-a-kind stuffed hedgehog at the toy store in time for her school's holiday pageant. But every time she visits him in the store she passes a homeless man sitting on the sidewalk. As her earnings to buy the toy grow, so does her distress at the man's plight. She makes a decision that brightens the holidays for herself and others. The book offers a good look at varying attitudes toward homeless people.

♥ *Tails of the Bronx* by Jill Pinkwater. Simon & Schuster, 1991. 3–5. The kids of Burnridge Avenue have a mystery to solve—neighborhood cats are disappearing. The prime suspect is the local witch! In this straightforward yet complex novel about the realities and creative potential of coping in a poor urban neighborhood, nothing is as it seems. But the kids and their tightly knit families pull together to make life safer and better for the kids, the cats, the "witch" and a pair of homeless people. A story full of "tough kid" dialogue, quirky characters, humor and heart.

♥ *Uncle Willie and the Soup Kitchen* by DyAnne DiSalvo-Ryan. William Morrow & Co., 1997. K–3. A young boy gets a close-up look at community caring in action when he goes to help at the soup kitchen where his uncle works.

Nonfiction

♥ *Erik is Homeless* by Keith Elliot Greenberg. Lerner Publications, 1992. 3–4. Using black-and-white photos, this picture book tells about life for Erik and his mother Lydia, who are homeless. They have experienced the worst of the shelters and welfare hotels and now live in a facility that provides services to help them transition to an apartment, school and job. The text maintains an objective tone while ending on a hopeful note. Passing references to the harsh realities of drug dealing, prostitution, condoms, etc., may make this title inappropriate for the youngest students.

♥ *Home: A Collaboration of Thirty Distinguished Authors and Illustrators of Children's Books to Aid the Homeless* edited by Michael Rosen. HarperCollins, 1996. K–5. Proceeds from this lovely picture book, made up of poems, vignettes and lush illustrations by some of the brightest talents creating for children, go to support Share Our Strength (SOS), which aids the hungry and homeless. As we learn about homelessness, we also deepen our appreciation of what home means to us.

♥ *Homeless Children* by Eleanor H. Ayer. Lucent Books, 1996. 4–5. This Lucent Overview series title takes a broad look at the history, causes and realities of and attitudes toward homelessness for children in America. While the outlook is grim, the book provides useful information and examines government and private social or charitable programs working to help homeless children. An appendix suggests ways young people can get involved.

♥ *Jane Addams: Nobel Prize Winner and Founder of Hull House* by Bonnie Carman Harvey. Enslow Publishers, 1999. 4–5. Despite a privileged background, Jane Addams knew from a very young age that she wanted to help the poor. This detailed, well-constructed biography explores the motivations and paths that led a remarkable woman to achieving her remarkable goals. Harvey reveals her periods of insecurity and the political positions that caused her popularity to wax and wane, along with the dedication and compassion of this true servant of humankind.

♥ *Working Together Against Homelessness* by Sue Hurwitz. Simon & Schuster, 1994. 3–5. Written with a more global perspective and for younger students than the Lucent Overview series, this Library of Social Activism title also provides background and context about the problem of homelessness in America. It features conversations with homeless people and with others trying to help through involvement in local organizations and initiatives. Dialogue doesn't always ring true, as a fictional sixth grade class pursues an assignment to complete individual service projects. Chapters end with questions intended for reflection.

♥ *World Hunger* by Liza N. Burby. Lucent Books, 1994. 4–5. Another in the Lucent Overview series, this book concentrates on conditions and responses to hunger in "the hunger belt," which consists of much of the Southern Hemisphere. Dramatic black-and-white photos illustrate the suffering caused by hunger while the text ends on a cautiously hopeful note, claiming that we now have the resources to end world hunger forever. While exposure to the world's hunger crisis may be overwhelming to some students, it is critical to create a global context and to encourage global responsibility for the problem in addition to supporting local involvement.

Other Media

♥ *Fly Away Home* by Eve Bunting. Columbia Tristar, 1996 (videocassette). K–4. This Reading Rainbow episode features Bunting's sad and touching story of a young boy and his father who live in an airport while they look for work and save money for a home. Program host LeVar Burton talks with homeless children and families about their experiences, and with young people helping to fight the battle against homelessness.

♥ *Gracie's Girl* by Ellen Wittlinger, narrated by Stina Nielsen. Recorded Books, 2002 (audiocassettes). 4–5. Eleven-year-old Bess starts middle school with two things on her mind—how to be popular at school and how to claim more attention from her social activist mother who seems too busy helping others to notice her. Bess and her friend Ethan get involved in the school play and then meet Gracie, a homeless old woman who touches them and needs their help. A lovely, well-written story of appealing young people finding a social conscience and claiming a place in their world.

Web sites

♥ *The Hunger Site*
www.thehungersite.com

♥ *The National Coalition for the Homeless*
www.nationalhomeless.org
Check out "Facts about Homelessness" and "K–12 Educational Materials" (including "Kids Corner").

♥ *Think Quest*
library.thinkquest.org
You'll find several good sites on homelessness and several on hunger. Search the Library for "hunger" and "homeless."

Service-Learning in Action

The following examples tell of service-learning projects in which elementary students joined the battle against hunger and homelessness in their local communities.

♥ **Empty Bowls, Marion, Iowa**

Adopting an idea that originated in Michigan in 1991, high school art teacher Barb Shultz of Marion, Iowa, introduced the Empty Bowls project as part of the high school art curriculum in 1996. Since 1997, high school art students have worked with Marion's third graders on the project. In the project, third grade students, under the direction of elementary art teacher Michele Weisinger, are aided by high school art students to create ceramic bowls. Bowls made by both third graders and high school students are displayed at the annual Marion Arts Festival, where they are sold to benefit local food pantries. In 2000, the project won the Iowa Health Prize and was awarded $5,000 by the Farm Bureau to supplement proceeds. At the time of this writing Marion art students have earned over $33,000 and donated all of it to local food banks! For more information on Empty Bowls, contact:

> Barb Shultz
> 319-377-9891
> bshultz@marion.k12.ia.us
> www.emptybowls.net

♥ **Common Cents, New York, New York**

In New York City in 1991 a young girl named Nora Gross and her father, Teddy Gross, came upon a homeless man in the street. Nora wanted to invite him home and help him! Instead, the two decided to gather some friends and collect pennies to provide needed supplies for a local homeless shelter. From that small but inspiring beginning came Common Cents, an organization that now implements service-learning initiatives in 940 New York City K–12 schools and proves to countless young people that they can make a difference. The fall "penny harvest" is still at the heart of the organization's activities and participating students have a voice in where the grants based on that "harvest" go. In 2002 alone, students raised over $720,000, mostly in pennies! The organization's Web site (www.commoncents.org) will tell you more about the program, grant recipients to date and plans for the future. The site also offers a Roundtable Handbook, which you can download free of charge. Contact the organization directly at:

> Common Cents
> Attn. Teddy Gross
> 570 Columbus Avenue
> New York, NY 10024
> 212-579-0579
> info@commoncents.org

♥ **Weights and Measures, Palo Alto, California**

In 1995, second graders at Ohlone Elementary School in Palo Alto, California, were completing a unit on weights and measures. Nelda Brown and Kent Koth, consultants for a nonprofit organization called Youth Community Service, put the school in touch with the Urban Ministry Food Closet, which had a problem. They had 100-pound sacks of rice and not enough staff to sort and package the rice into family-sized portions for distribution. Brown and Koth took the rice to the school, introduced the children to the needs of the poor and hungry and explained the project. Being careful not to spill the precious food and using measuring cups in a variety of sizes, teams of students sorted the rice into 1-cup packages. Further suggestions for using this activity with first or second graders are offered at the State Education Agency Web site (www.seanetonline.org). Click on "practice of service-learning in schools," then on "Service-Learning in Action."

Activities on Hunger and the Homeless

Discussion Prompts

Use the following prompts to explore issues of hunger and homelessness.

♥ **Who Are the Homeless?** Consider homeless characters from the books in this chapter's bibliography. How did they come to be homeless? Were they lazy, irresponsible or "crazy"? Were they criminals or addicted to alcohol or drugs? Do you think homelessness is something that could happen to anyone?

♥ **Hunger and Homelessness Here.** Do you think there are hungry or homeless people in your town? In your neighborhood? In your school community?
Note: Teachers, this is important ground to cover, but proceed carefully. You may discover that there are homeless children in your school, or even in your class, who are embarrassed and secretive about their plight. Do all you can to protect the privacy, pride and dignity of these children and work with your school counselors or administrators as appropriate.

♥ **How Would it Feel?** How do you think it might feel to go to bed hungry at night? To have to sleep in a shelter with no privacy, or even on the street? To have only the possessions you could carry with you? What would you miss most about the way your life is now?

Games

♥ **Matching Game.** Hand out the reproducible matching game on page 15, based on words and phrases related to hunger and homelessness. The answers are: G, I, L, D, F, N, H, K, E, O, A, J, B, C and M.

♥ **Empathy Tag.** This empathy-building game can be going on quietly in the background of normal classroom activity. Prepare a long, thin scroll (4¼" x 11") with writing lines. At the top, write "If I didn't have a home I would feel _____ because _____." Set the tone by writing your brief response on the top line. Do not sign your name. Roll up the scroll and secure it with a rubber band or ribbon. Explain the process and "tag" a student by giving him or her the scroll. That student will

think about a response and write it on the next line. At an appropriate time, e.g., a transition between activities or lessons, that student will "tag" another student who hasn't already had a turn by giving him or her the scroll. In this way the scroll will make its way through the class giving everyone a turn. Clarify that students should take time to think about their responses and not let the game interrupt the day's work. It might take a day, a week or longer to complete the game. When each student has contributed to the scroll, share it by reading it aloud, posting it in the classroom or adding it to a learning center.

Creative Expressions

Enjoy these creative ways to process concepts from the books on the list.

♥ **Personal Expressions.** Review the book *Home: A Collaboration of Thirty Distinguished Authors and Illustrators of Children's Books to Aid the Homeless* or read Chapter 7 of *Sophie and the Sidewalk Man* and reflect on what "home" means to characters in other books on the list. Then have students write their own poems or essays about what "home" means to them.

♥ **Classroom Display.** Assign students to bring in magazine or newspaper articles and illustrations about hunger and homelessness. Then create a classroom display that reflects student understanding of the issues. Students might decorate the display with their own drawings or appropriate words added "graffiti style."

♥ **Myth Making.** *I Can Hear the Sun* is described as a myth, which means a story that contains supernatural or fantasy elements that help us understand or deal with something puzzling about our world. Invite students to try writing myths that either explain why there is hunger and homelessness in the world or, as in *I Can Hear the Sun,* that show someone being magically rescued from trials because of his or her goodness or innocence.

♥ **Creative Expression.** Building on the discussion prompt How Would it Feel?, and based on readings from this chapter, have students imagine themselves in the place of a hungry or homeless child and draw a picture, write a journal entry or create a poem or song about how it might feel to be hungry or homeless. You might start by reviewing *Someplace to Go*.

Research Opportunities

♥ **Causes of Homelessness.** Have students use books from the chapter bibliography and other classroom, media center or public library resources to research the main causes of homelessness in America. Use the worksheet on page 16 to help students organize their findings and ideas. From the organizers, students will create posters to share the results of their research. *Working Together Against Homelessness* and *Homeless Children* are good places to start.

♥ **Vietnam Veterans.** Several books in this chapter bibliography (*Darnell Rock Reporting, The King of Dragons, Anna Casey's Place in the World, I Can Hear the Sun*) include homeless characters who are veterans of the Vietnam War. Invite interested students to find out whether there really are many Vietnam War veterans among the homeless and to explore reasons why that might be. Along with searching print and electronic sources, students might talk to their parents or grandparents for ideas, ask people who work for organizations that help the homeless and check with the local Department of Veterans Affairs. Students should report their findings to the class.

♥ **The Foster Care System.** Other books on the list *(Sammy Keyes and the Sisters of Mercy, The King of Dragons, Tails of the Bronx)* have characters trying to avoid police or government agencies due to fear of, or bad experiences with, foster care. Have students talk to representatives of the foster care system and research their goals and achievements; successes and failures; and the challenges they face as they try to help homeless children and families.

Miscellaneous Activities

♥ **Success Stories.** Can you identify a "success story" in your community—someone who was once homeless or living with hunger and managed to regain economic stability? It might be fascinating, enlightening and empathy-building to invite such a person to visit the class and share his or her experience openly and honestly. Prepare the class to ask appropriate, respectful questions.

♥ **Field Trip.** Arrange a field trip to visit a food pantry, soup kitchen or homeless shelter in your community. Prepare students who may be surprised by evidence of poverty that they are not used to seeing. You might discuss in advance some sample questions to ask that will help them make the most of their visit while showing respect for staff and clients.

♥ **Experiencing Hunger.** Many students have never felt real hunger. Invite students to experience a "taste" of hunger by volunteering to skip snacks and lunch between breakfast and dinner one day. This voluntary deprivation should produce just enough physical hunger to raise awareness; it should not be allowed to compromise any student's health. You might introduce this experience with a letter to parents, explaining your studies and the goal of building empathy for the less fortunate, and including a statement by the school nurse addressing any related health concerns. You might follow up by discussing how students felt during their self-imposed fast and how it affected their ability think, work and play.

Hunger and Homelessness Right Here

In Your Community

Use these starting points to discover needs and activity in your local community.

- ♥ Check out the phone book. Look in the yellow pages under headings like "Homeless Services," "Human Services" and "Social Service Organizations." Check government pages under "Health and Human Services" or "Social Services."

- ♥ Call your city hall or county supervisor's office and ask what services are provided for the hungry and homeless, and what organizations in the community work to help them.

- ♥ Check out SERVEnet (www.servenet.org) to see what organizations that serve the hungry or homeless are listed for your area.

- ♥ Watch local newspapers and other publications for articles on hunger and homelessness in your community.

- ♥ Talk to people "in the know" on this subject. They might be government employees or directors of community service agencies like shelters or food pantries. You might invite such resource people to visit the class or assign students to practice communication, research and presentation skills by interviewing appropriate people and reporting back. Find out what these experts feel are the greatest needs in the local community.
  Note: Don't overlook the school community! Your principal, counselor, nurse or other school staff may have ideas of needs within the school district that could use some attention.

- ♥ Brainstorm about other ways you might identify needs of the hungry and homeless in your community.

Taking Action

Based on your research about hunger and homelessness in your community, make a plan for your service-learning project. These ideas might help you start generating suggestions for making a difference "in the real world."

- ♥ Organize a food drive for a local soup kitchen or food pantry.

- ♥ Stock shelves or take inventory at a local food pantry.

- ♥ Find out what your local shelter needs for supplies and collect those items to donate.

- ♥ Raise money to help support operating costs or provide bigger-ticket items for a local organization that helps the hungry or homeless.

- ♥ Invite homeless children from a local shelter to join the class on a field trip.

- ♥ Create a petition, letter to the editor or letter-writing campaign to political officials in support of improved services for the homeless and hungry, and carry it out as a class.

- ♥ Produce a TV or radio public service announcement advocating the needs of the hungry or homeless in your community.

More Ideas

Offer these ideas to motivated students who want to help as individuals.

- ♥ Ask your parents to help you visit a homeless shelter or to assist at a soup kitchen or food pantry.

- ♥ Volunteer as a tutor, homework helper or "read aloud" resource for homeless kids.

- ♥ Talk to your parents about befriending a homeless person or inviting a homeless child along on a family outing.

- ♥ Ask your parents to help you volunteer for an organization that collects leftover food from restaurants to feed the hungry.

- ♥ Keep learning about the issues and expressing your informed views to your local paper, local government officials and national politicians.

Hunger and Homelessness Matching Game

Write the letter from the list on the right that matches the definitions on the left.

_____ A cause of homelessness is not enough well-paid _____.

_____ A person with no place to live is called _____.

_____ Some hungry people search for food in _____.

_____ A "Penny _____" is a way to raise funds to help the homeless.

_____ You feel _____ when you don't have enough to eat.

_____ "Homeless _____" house many homeless people in small rooms or apartments in one building.

_____ A cause of homelessness is not enough low-cost _____.

_____ A homeless _____ provides beds for the homeless.

_____ Subsidized means paid for partly with _____ funds.

_____ Another name for food bank is food _____.

_____ People with too little money to support themselves are said to live in _____.

_____ It's important to protect the _____ of hungry or homeless people.

_____ _____ is government assistance for the poor or hungry.

_____ A "soup _____" offers free food to the hungry.

_____ The process of moving from homelessness back to a stable job and home.

A. poverty

B. welfare

C. kitchen

D. harvest

E. public

F. hunger

G. jobs

H. housing

I. homeless

J. dignity

K. shelter

L. dumpsters

M. transition

N. hotels

O. pantry

Causes of Homelessness

Organize the ideas you discover in your research on the causes of homelessness by writing them in the appropriate circles below. For each cause of homelessness you discover, write an idea or two for addressing the problem in the connecting circle. An example has been done for you. You may want to add your own ideas to those in the sample circle.

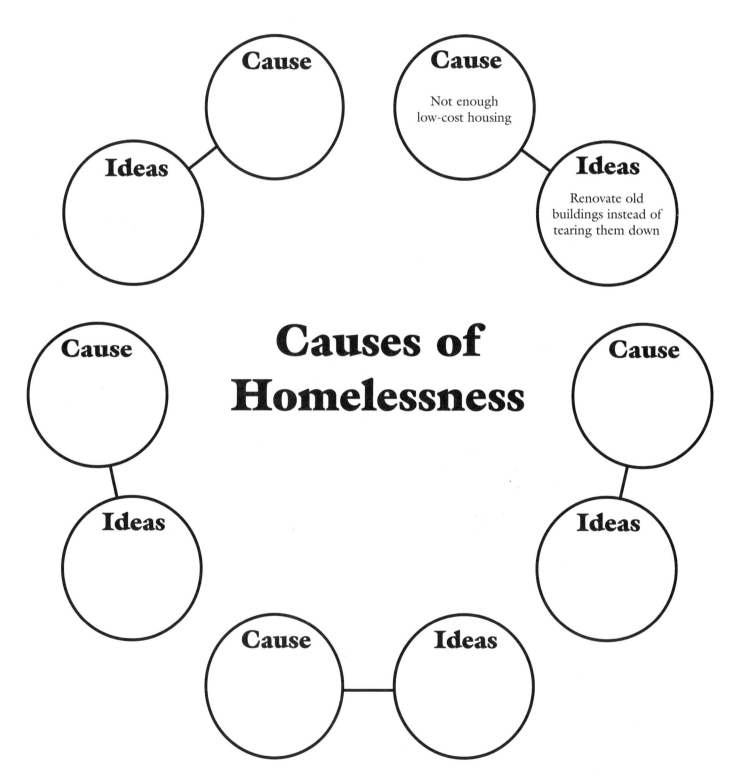

Animal Welfare

Whether we live in the city or the country, animals are part of our lives. Many of us have pets. We listen to the singing of birds, eat meat or other animal products, wear leather or fur, visit zoos and use products or take medicines that involve animals in their preparation or testing. Some of us ride horses or hunt and fish for sport. All of us benefit from animals in ways we never stop to consider. For example, scavenger fish and carrion birds help keep our land and water clean. Toads and lizards keep insect populations in check. A whole host of animals fertilize the soil that grows the plants we eat. Learning to appreciate and care for the animals that share the earth with us is important in itself, apart from the imperative to address problems of animal welfare that can intrude in our lives.

Addressing these problems and learning to care for animals raise complex ethical questions about the relationship of humans to animals and to the natural world. People hold a wide range of opinions about those relationships. At one extreme, some consider all forms of life on the planet equal and deserving of equal rights and protection. At the other extreme, some see humans as masters of the earth with the right to exploit animals as we see fit. Most fall somewhere in between, viewing animals as deserving of care and compassion but holding an inferior position to humans in the grand scheme of things. Whether we have pondered our own stands on these issues or not, we make decisions every day that impact the lives of animals. What we eat, what products we buy, what leisure activities we enjoy, how we care for our pets—all of these choices have consequences for animals.

What are the issues of animal welfare in our communities, and how can we address them? These topics might help focus your study of animal welfare.

- ♥ Are humans superior to animals?

- ♥ Rights and protection for animals.

- ♥ Do some species of animals deserve more care and concern than others? Is it more acceptable to kill or endanger animals for food or medicines than for luxury or entertainment?

- ♥ Attitudes toward companion animals, domestic animals, wild animals or endangered animals.

- ♥ Services provided by animals.

- ♥ How has human behavior disrupted the lives of animals?

- ♥ Endangered and overpopulated species.

- ♥ The animal rights vs. animal welfare movements—similarities and differences.

- ♥ What organizations promote each of these movements?

Resources on Animal Welfare

Use these resources to build knowledge and stimulate involvement in issues of animal welfare.

♥ Fiction

♥ **Condor's Egg** by Jonathan London. Chronicle Books, 1999. K–5. This beautiful picture book shows a pair of condors soaring through the sky, cleaning up the earth and tending a nest. An endnote summarizes the plight of the endangered condor at the time of publication and efforts to save the species. A good tool for instilling respect for nature's wild creatures.

♥ **If Anything Ever Goes Wrong at the Zoo** by Mary Jean Hendrick. Harcourt Brace, 1993. K–3. Leslie loves the zoo! She tells the zookeepers, "If anything ever goes wrong…" they can bring the animals to stay at her house. But none of them come, until one night…. A sweet, silly look at what conditions and care different animals need in order to thrive.

♥ **Mr. Popper's Penguins** by Richard and Florence Atwater. Little, Brown and Company, 1992. 2–4. Newbery Honor Book. In this hilarious story, Mr. Popper receives the gift of a penguin from Antarctica and his family's life is turned upside down. Tucked into the delightful nonsense is considerable information about penguins, their lives and needs.

♥ **One Day at Wood Green Animal Shelter** by Patricia Casey. Candlewick Press, 2001. K–5. In an eye-catching montage of words, drawings and photo images, Casey surrounds us with the busy sights and sounds of a typical day at a real animal shelter and clinic. A wonderful introduction to the work and needs of multipurpose shelters.

♥ **Saving Lilly** by Peg Kehret. Pocket Books, 2001. 3–5. Sixth graders Erin and David learn about the common mistreatment of circus animals in their TAG program. When their sixth grade teacher announces a trip to a visiting circus as the reward for a successful class project the two protest, but their teacher is determined that everyone will attend. The plot thickens when Erin and David discover that Lilly, the circus elephant, is indeed being abused and neglected. Can a couple of students lead a successful protest and save Lilly in the process?

♥ **Shiloh** by Phyllis Reynolds Naylor. Aladdin Paperbacks, 2000. 3–5. Newbery Medal Book. Rural West Virginia is the setting for this award-winning drama. Eleven-year-old Marty, whose family can't afford a pet, befriends a dog mistreated by its owner. He hides the dog, setting off a series of lies and conflicts that torment his developing conscience. As he faces the consequences of his actions and the complicated questions they raise, Marty finds courage and growth in himself and earns the respect of others. An outstanding look at a very complex ethical landscape.

♥ **Throw-Away Pets** by Betsy Duffey. Penguin Putnam, 1995. 2–4. This title in The Pet Patrol series has Evie and Megan discovering three "throw-away" pets doomed to be euthanized as unadoptable. Can they save the day? The easy-to-read story offers engaging characters and a look at the fate of abandoned pets. Other series titles, *Puppy Love* and *Wild Things,* offer similar light glimpses of kids standing up for animals.

♥ **Tiger Rising** by Kate DiCamillo. Candlewick Press, 2002. 5+. In this dreamlike, haunting story two outcast sixth graders, both carrying huge burdens of emotional pain, find a tiger caged in the woods. The tiger represents to the children everything powerful and beautiful that has been locked up within them by their sad life experiences. Freeing the tiger, even with its disastrous consequences, frees them to accept the realities of their lives and move forward. A sophisticated look at animals as symbols for mature readers.

♥ **The Trouble with Zinny Weston** by Amy Goldman Koss. Dial Books for Young Readers, 1998. 3–5. Ava and Zinny are best friends. They get along great in spite of the fact that Zinny's family hates animals and Ava's family are all animal fanatics. Then cruelty to an animal precipitates a crisis in their friendship. A light, fun read that raises important questions about animal welfare and our attitudes toward it.

♥ **Unknown** by Colin Thompson. Walker & Company, 2000. K–3. "Unknown" is the least conspicuous animal at the shelter. While others beg people to "take me, take me," she cowers in a corner. But when fire breaks out at the shelter, it's Unknown who saves the day, with surprising results all around. A sweet and visually rich picture book experience.

♥ **The Wolves** by Brian J. Heinz. Penguin Putnam, 1996. K–5. This lovely, dreamlike picture book tells the fate that wolves of North America face because of human interference with their native habitat. It follows a hungry pack through an elk hunt, instilling understanding and respect for the benign, if sometimes harsh, balance of weak and strong in nature.

♥ **Wringer** by Jerry Spinelli. HarperCollins, 1998. 4–5. Newbery Honor Book, ALA Notable Children's Book. This award winner is a disturbing story of a young boy caught between his feelings and the cruel expectations of a long-standing community tradition. Each year his town concludes its big family celebration with a contest to see who can shoot the most pigeons. Ten-year-old boys serve as "wringers," wringing the necks of birds that are wounded but not killed. Palmer doesn't want to be a wringer, but also dreads being labeled a coward and ostracized by his peers. His dilemma is magnified when a stray pigeon befriends him. Not for all students, but mature readers will find much to think about as Palmer struggles with fears, feelings, belief and courage.

♥ **Zucchini Out West** by Barbara Dana. HarperCollins, 1997. 3–5. Billy and his pet ferret Zucchini are best friends. Billy is shy around people, but he cares a lot about animals and the environment, and the endangered black-footed ferret in particular. When Billy's father takes him out West to visit the ferrets' natural habitat and meet the biologists who study them, Billy comes face to face with both his fears and his hopes. Appealing, unusual characters and a close-up look at an endangered animal and the people who try to protect it make this light read memorable.

Nonfiction

♥ **Animal Rights** by Barbara James. Raintree Publishers, 1999. 3–5. Chapters on food and farming, animal experiments, animals in entertainment, hunting, pets and exploitation and extinction spell out the main issues and arguments about animal rights in this Talking Points series title. The tone is balanced, with lots of questions posed for reflection and discussion. An excellent title to engage students and stimulate response.

♥ **The Black-Footed Ferret** by Alvin and Virginia Silverstein and Laura Silverstein Nunn. Millbrook Press, 1995. 4–5. This well written, visually appealing Endangered In America series title shares the history and life of the black-footed ferret and its journey toward, and then back from, the brink of extinction. An interesting read with lots of photos and sidebars. Other titles in the series include *The Spotted Owl, The Peregrine Falcon, The Red Wolf, The Manatee* and *The Sea Otter*.

♥ **The Crocodile Hunter: The Incredible Life and Adventures of Steve and Terri Irwin** by Steve and Terri Irwin. Dutton/Plume, 2001. 3–5. Popular TV celebrities Steve and Terri Irwin tell of Steve's unique childhood sharing his parents' passion for Australian reptiles, and of their life work carrying on the family legacy of conservation and wildlife preservation at the Australia Zoo. The chatty, hyper-energetic tone full of Aussie dialect will be familiar to fans of the Irwins and should be an easy sell!

♥ **Endangered Animal Babies: Saving Species One Birth at a Time** by Thane Maynard. Franklin Watts, 1993. K–5. Twenty-eight endangered species are featured in attractive two-page spreads in this informative picture book. Full-page color photos and lots of concise information make this a great "first stop" for generating interest or starting research on specific species. While the 1993 copyright dates the information, it might motivate students to follow up on the fate of specific animals since that time.

♥ **The Humane Societies: A Voice for the Animals** by Shelley Swanson Sataren. Silver Burdett Press, 1996. K–5. This excellent, highly informative little book presents a basic overview on problems of animal welfare in America and the organizations that tackle those problems. Many color photos and an appealing layout make it accessible and easy to use with all ages.

♥ **Shelter Dogs: Amazing Stories of Adopted Strays** by Peg Kehret. Albert Whitman & Company, 1999. 4–5. The eight shelter dogs featured in this book all seemed like long shots for adoption—too old, too big, too nervous…. But each found a loving home and went on to do extraordinary things. Along with fun and uplifting stories, Kehret offers information about pet care, safety and organizations that work with companion animals.

Other Media

♥ *Discovery Channel: Animal Planet—Sing with the Animals.* Rhino Records, 1998 (CD). K–2. This delightfully silly collection of songs about animals includes both original recordings like "See You Later, Alligator" by Bill Haley and His Comets and hilarious remakes like "Born to be Wild" by Chickenwolf (Yes, you read that correctly!). You might use it as background music or to lighten the mood as you deal with the chapter's heavy issues.

♥ *Love Me, Love My Broccoli* by Julie Anne Peters, narrated by Julie Dretzin. Recorded Books, 2002 (audiocassettes). 4–5. Chloe's an eighth grade animal rights activist who finds herself losing sight of her convictions when a handsome jock chooses her as his girlfriend. Conflicting priorities in Chloe's life reach a crisis point and she is forced to reevaluate what's important. The developing romance and a sprinkling of objectionable language make this light but sophisticated story best for more mature students.

♥ *On the Far Side of the Mountain* by Jean Craighead George, narrated by Jeff Woodman. Recorded Books, 1995. 4–5. This sequel to the award-winning *My Side of the Mountain* has Sam's sister Alice joining him on the mountain. The plot concerns Sam's peregrine falcon Frightful, who is confiscated under laws protecting endangered species. It's a wonderful adventure story, full of details about wilderness living and new awareness for Sam about animal abuse and respecting wild creatures.

Web sites

♥ *American Humane Association "Just for Kids"* www.americanhumane.org/kids/ The AHA home page offers an introduction to "free farmed food" which spells out animal welfare issues related to livestock farming.

♥ *American Veterinary Medical Association Care for Pets "Kid's Corner"* www.avma.org/careforanimals/kidscorner/

♥ *Kids' Planet by Defenders of Wildlife* www.kidsplanet.org Includes curriculum on several endangered species and information about adopting an endangered animal in the teacher's section.

♥ *PETA Kids* www.peta.org/kids This site, sponsored by the animal rights organization People for the Ethical Treatment of Animals, stresses vegetarianism, opposing dissection in schools and other animal rights issues.

♥ *Think Quest* library.thinkquest.org You'll find many good sites dealing with animal welfare issues. A few particularly interesting ones are: ES2000—Endangered Species of the Next Millennium, The Virtual Zoo and The Octopus Garden. Search the Library for "animal welfare" or one of the specific titles.

Service-Learning in Action

Here are some examples of service-learning projects in which elementary students took action to protect animals in their communities.

♥ **Special Education Students Adopt Animal Shelter, Hanford, California**

In the fall of 2001 Special Education teacher Carla Lewis, at Shelly Baird School in Hanford, California, picked up on cues in her classroom related to the web of life and our responsibilities to take care of each other, and her students' love for animals. She created a unit on pets, which stimulated students to develop a plan to adopt the local SPCA (Society for the Prevention of Cruelty to Animals) animal shelter. Susan Withers, manager of the shelter, was enthusiastic and Principal Barbara Zaino suggested a school-wide effort led by the Special Education class. The local newspaper covered the project and parents were invited to help. Each class designed a "Help the SPCA" contributions jar and created its own plans for assisting the shelter. The shelter provided a doghouse to serve as a collection point for donations of pet food, cat litter, towels and other needed supplies.

Lewis' class of eleven 6–13-year-old special needs students ran a concession stand for two months, donating a portion of the proceeds to the SPCA. They incorporated counting and rolling coins, and banking and shopping trips, into their math curriculum. They took their turns delivering donated items to the shelter, where they took a tour to see how the animals live. Students found this so motivating that they eagerly brought in handfuls of change for their classroom jar throughout the entire school year!

Lewis plans to continue the project, involving community businesses in the 2002–03 school year. To learn more about this project contact:
Carla Lewis
559-584-5546
clewis@kings.k12.ca.us

♥ **Keep the Change Project, Bowling Green, Kentucky**

In March of 2001 about 25 students from T. C. Cherry Elementary School in Bowling Green, Kentucky, who participated in the school's after-school program operated by Bowling Green/Warren County Community Education, helped support the local Humane Society. Students learned about the importance of spaying and neutering pets and wanted to do something about it. Program supervisor Jamie Lancaster and other group leaders supervised as students made eye-catching collection containers and placed them in local businesses. They also contributed change of their own and accepted donations of needed supplies for the Humane Society. The children sorted and counted the change, reinforcing math skills. Character education was also emphasized, as students learned about responsibility and helped teach the community about the problem of unwanted pets. Proceeds went to offer discounted spay and neuter services for local pet owners. For more information, contact:
Jamie Lancaster
lancasterjamie@hotmail.com
Bowling Green/Warren County
Community Education office
270-842-4281

Activities on Animal Welfare

Discussion Prompts

Use these prompts to explore issues of animal welfare.

♥ **Stocking an Animal Shelter.** Review *One Day at Wood Green Animal Shelter*. Based on the book (look carefully at the illustrations), lead a brainstorming session on supplies that an animal shelter and clinic might need. Encourage everything from pet food to basic office supplies—even shredded newspaper! Then discuss ideas about how the class might provide some of those supplies.

♥ **Book Discussions.** Assign older readers to one of three groups. One group will read *Shiloh*, one *Wringer* and one will read or listen to *On the Far Side of the Mountain*. After reading their books, each group will discuss what the book had to say about animal welfare, using these prompts:

- Describe the relationship between the main character and the animal in the book.

- What dangers or hardships does the animal face?

- What responsibility does the main character feel toward the animal?

- How is the animal welfare issue resolved in the story?

- What new ideas did you take from the story about the relationship between people and animals?

♥ **Debate.** Assign individuals or teams to debate affirmative and negative positions on animal welfare resolutions. They will research their topics (*Animal Rights* and *The Humane Societies* are good starting points), then present arguments and rebuttals. The class might vote by show of hands to determine which side was more convincing. These ideas will get you started. Add your own or let students suggest other resolutions.

- Only animals that directly serve people (pets, service or domestic animals) deserve protection and humane treatment.

- It is ethical to kill animals for food but not for entertainment or luxury.

- Pets will live better, more natural lives if they're allowed to reproduce.

- Animals deserve equal rights and protection to humans.

- People and the earth would be better off if we were all vegetarians.

Games

Use these when you need a pleasant break in the day's work.

♥ **Crossword Puzzle.** Enjoy the crossword puzzle on page 25, using words and phrases that relate to animal welfare. If might be helpful to provide a word bank. The answers are:

Across	Down
3. companion	1. feline
5. canine	2. sanctuary
7. domestic	4. welfare
9. endangered	6. wild
10. extinct	8. rights
11. spay	9. euthanize
12. veterinarian	13. neuter
14. dissect	
15. humane	

♥ **Beastly Musical Chairs.** Set up a game of musical chairs using the *Animal Planet—Sing with the Animals* CD. Play clips of several songs, jumping from track to track. When the music stops, students without chairs must draw pictures of an animal named or suggested in the last song played. First and second grade students might also caption their pictures with basic information about the animal and where or how it lives.

Creative Expressions

Enjoy these creative ways to process concepts from books on the list.

♥ **Save Endangered Animals!** Using books in the chapter bibliography as a starting point, have students choose an endangered animal

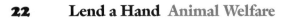

and create a "Save the ___" poster to convince people to learn about the importance of the animal. You might display the posters in the classroom, lunchroom or hallway.

♥ **Animal Puppets.** Using felt in different colors, pipe cleaners, scissors, glue and craft sticks, make puppets of animals you might see in a zoo or circus. Then have students write or record brief speeches, in the voices of their animal puppets, telling about their natural habitat and how they live in the wild. Then take turns having the animal puppets give their speeches to the class. To add challenge and build empathy, invite students to have their animal puppets comment on how they feel about living in a zoo or circus environment.

♥ **Fiction/Nonfiction Book Reports.** *Zucchini Out West* and *The Black-Footed Ferret* deal with the same endangered animal. Each book offers different insights about the animal. Have students choose a fiction title from the bibliography that features a particular animal. Then have them find a nonfiction book about the same animal to read and compare. Have students present brief book reports on their pairs of books, conveying what they learned about the animal and what different facts and feelings each book contributed to their knowledge.

Research Opportunities

♥ **Endangered Animals.** Invite students to research a particular endangered animal. You might define a geographical focus as large as the world or as small as your state. Students should create reports or displays that tell where their animal lives, its social structure, what it eats, its current level of danger of extinction and what is being done to protect it. In a simpler version, you might start with *Endangered Animal Babies* and have students update the information from 1993. To identify endangered species in your state, contact the Department of Natural Resources or check out the EndangeredSpecie.com Web site (www.endangeredspecie.com), which lists endangered animals by state.

♥ **Animal Rights vs. Animal Welfare Movements.** Have students compare and contrast the goals and beliefs of the animal welfare movement with the animal rights movement, using the reproducible graphic organizer on page 26. Again, *Animal Rights* and *The Humane Societies* would be good starting points. As a follow-up, you might invite an activist from each group to visit the class and answer students' questions that arise from the research.

♥ **Persuasive Speeches.** If you have students who are passionate about animal rights, invite them to prepare persuasive speeches that "make their cases" about animal research and testing, factory farms, eating animal products or whatever issues most interest them. Insist that the speeches be well researched and documented.

Miscellaneous Activities

♥ **Do the Math.** Based on information found in *The Humane Societies* about cat gestation and litter size, introduce the mathematical concept of geometric progression by having students figure out how many cats could be produced in a year, starting with one unspayed female.

♥ **Pet Show-and-Tell.** Invite students to bring their pets to show. Have them explain what they gain from having a pet, how they care for its needs and what they do to be responsible pet owners.

♥ **Field Trip.** Arrange a field trip to visit a reputable zoo, livestock farm, veterinary clinic or animal shelter. Ask a member of the staff to talk to the class about what they do to promote animal welfare.

Animal Welfare Right Here

In Your Community

Use these starting points to discover needs and activity in your local community.

♥ Check out the phone book. Look in the yellow pages under headings like "Animal Rescue, Relocate & Transport," "Animal Shelters" and "Humane Societies." Check government listings under "Animal Control" or "Department of Natural Resources."

♥ Call your city hall or county supervisor's office and ask what agencies work with animal control or welfare and what community organizations help.

♥ Search SERVEnet (www.servenet.org) for organizations that promote animal welfare in your area.

♥ Watch the local newspapers and other publications for articles on how people and animals interact in your area.

♥ Talk to people "in the know" on this subject. They might be government employees, veterinarians or directors of service agencies like humane societies or zoos. You might invite such resource people to visit the class or assign students to practice communication, research and presentation skills by interviewing them and reporting back to the class. Find out what problems these people see that involve animals and what they think are the greatest needs in the community.

♥ Invite someone in your community who uses a service dog (review *Shelter Dogs* for ideas about different services dogs provide) to visit with his or her dog and explain how the animal helps and how it was trained. Is there anything your class might do to help make service dogs available to people who need them?

Taking Action

Based on your research about animal welfare issues in your community, develop a plan for your service-learning project. These ideas might help you start generating suggestions.

♥ Organize a drive to collect needed supplies for a local humane society.

♥ As a class, adopt an endangered animal through an organization that offers adoption programs (for details see the Kids' Planet Web site listed on page 20) or a zoo animal through a nearby zoo program.

♥ Visit an animal shelter as a class to help clean, stock supplies or socialize animals waiting for adoption.

♥ Raise money to help support operating costs, fund a "Free Neutering or Spaying" campaign or provide bigger-ticket items for a local organization that promotes animal welfare. You might try a raffle, craft or bake sale or "Dog Dash." (See *The Humane Societies* pages 19–22 for ideas.)

♥ Plan and present a course on responsible pet care for other classes in the school; perhaps develop and distribute a booklet on caring for common pets as part of the course.

♥ Wage a poster campaign at school encouraging students to save animal lives by spaying or neutering their pets.

♥ Create a petition, letter to the editor or letter-writing campaign to political officials in support of improved protection for endangered animals, and carry it out as a class.

More Ideas

Share these ideas with motivated students who want to help as individuals.

♥ Ask your parents to consider being a foster home for abandoned animals or to volunteer with you to use your pet in a local pet therapy program.

♥ Volunteer at a veterinarian's office or animal shelter cleaning up, grooming or socializing animals, or taking dogs through obedience training to make them more adoptable.

♥ Provide appropriate houses or food for birds native to your area.

♥ Make informed choices about what foods you eat, what products you buy and what entertainment you enjoy, based on the impact of those choices on animals.

♥ Keep learning about the issues and expressing your informed views to your local paper, local government officials and national politicians.

Animal Welfare Crossword Puzzle

Complete the crossword puzzle, using terms and phrases from your reading about animal welfare.

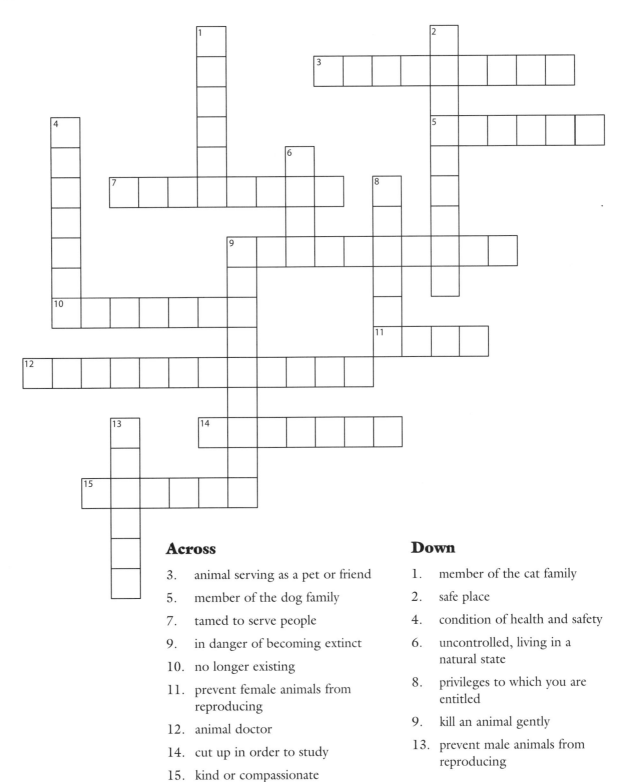

Across

3. animal serving as a pet or friend
5. member of the dog family
7. tamed to serve people
9. in danger of becoming extinct
10. no longer existing
11. prevent female animals from reproducing
12. animal doctor
14. cut up in order to study
15. kind or compassionate

Down

1. member of the cat family
2. safe place
4. condition of health and safety
6. uncontrolled, living in a natural state
8. privileges to which you are entitled
9. kill an animal gently
13. prevent male animals from reproducing

Compare and Contrast
Animal Rights and Animal Welfare Movements

Compare and contrast the goals and beliefs of the animal rights movement with the animal welfare movement. Write the goals and beliefs of each in the appropriate column. Then write the information that they share in the center column.

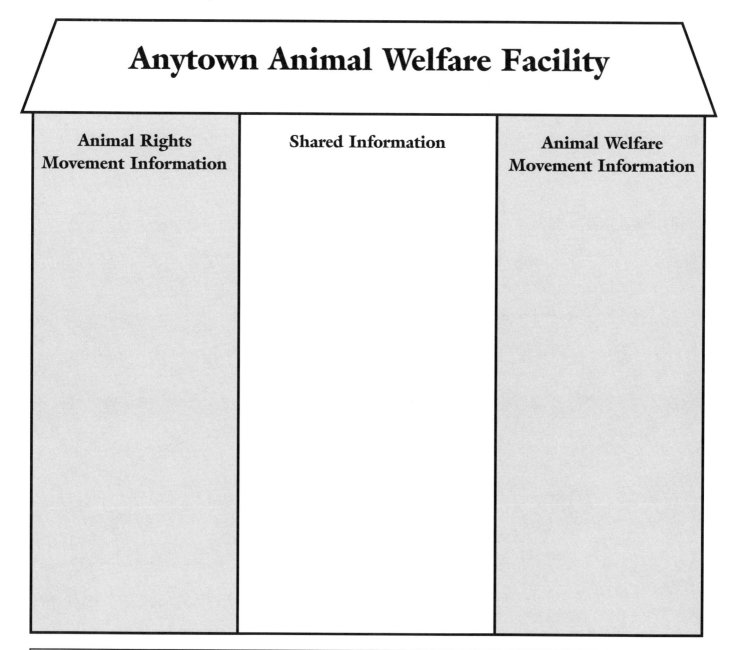

Anytown Animal Welfare Facility

Animal Rights Movement Information	Shared Information	Animal Welfare Movement Information

Based on your organizer, write a brief statement summarizing the similarities and differences between the two movements.

Health and Safety

Childhood has probably never been as carefree as we like to picture it in moments of adult nostalgia. Twenty-first century children in America will probably never experience polio or measles, and they have access to some of the best medical care in the world. But they may also be "latchkey kids" or "couch potatoes." They may suffer from obesity or eating disorders along with their elders, compromise their safety in Internet chat rooms or be at risk of AIDS simply by being born. All who deal with children share a responsibility to do what we can to protect their health and safety by encouraging good habits and preparing them for risks and dangers they may face. As we assess these good habits and risks we need to be sensitive to the emotional implications of body image, competitive attitudes, social pressures like teasing and dares, physical and mental illness, grief and loss—not just among our students, but throughout their families and friendship circles as well. Educating and encouraging our students to take good care of themselves and each other, and to contribute to health and safety in their communities, empowers them to meet daily challenges of their physical and emotional lives.

What issues of health and safety affect your community and how can you respond? Here are some topics to consider as you study issues of health and safety.

- ♥ Factors that contribute to good health.

- ♥ Services and facilities in your community that support good physical, mental and emotional health; accessing emergency services.

- ♥ What are the most common health problems in your community? The most common dangers (causes of illness or accidents, or sources of violence)?

- ♥ Natural disasters that occur in your area—how can you prepare for them?

- ♥ Impact of public health issues (smoking, obesity, substance abuse, etc.) on students' lives.

- ♥ How can children support each other's efforts to stay safe and deal with illness?

- ♥ Success stories—Who has tackled problems related to health and safety and succeeded in creating a safer, more wholesome community?

Resources on Health and Safety

Use these resources to explore issues of health and safety.

Fiction

♥ ***Anna and the Cat Lady*** by Barbara M. Joosse. HarperCollins, 1992. 2–5. Anna and Bethie's latest adventure lands them stranded in a basement with a stray kitten. Mrs. Sarafiny rescues them. Against parental advice, the girls befriend the strange woman. When Mrs. Sarafiny's increasingly weird and potentially dangerous behavior alarms the girls they risk punishment to get help. This humorous story sheds light on attitudes toward the mentally ill and ways children can help. It also brings together issues of hunger, animal welfare, health and safety.

♥ ***Arnie and the Skateboard Gang*** by Nancy Carlson. Viking Penguin, 1997. K–3. Arnie and Tina get good enough on their skateboards to join the cool kids at the park. But when the gang decides to try out a dangerous hill, Arnie has to decide how much he'll risk to be cool. A good "stand up for yourself" story.

♥ ***The Cow Buzzed*** by Andrea Zimmerman and David Clemesha. HarperCollins, 1993. K–3. A bee with a cold visits the barnyard and— "Ah-choo!"—spreads her sniffles to the cow, along with her buzz! The cold, and accompanying animal sounds, makes its way through the animal population creating a silly mix of coughs, sneezes, misplaced moos, oinks and quacks! Chaos continues until the animals figure out how to keep their germs to themselves.

♥ ***Diving for the Moon*** by Lee F. Bantle. Simon & Schuster, 1995. 4–5. Carolina "Bird" and Josh have spent summers together since they were babies, but their twelfth summer is different. Josh, who has hemophilia, tells Bird that he was infected with the HIV virus through tainted blood. A sweet story of friendship, fear, self-discovery and budding adolescence.

♥ ***Flapjack Waltzes*** by Nancy Hope Wilson. Farrar, Straus and Giroux, 1998. 3–5. Twelve-year-old Natalie's family is still reeling from the death of her brother in a car accident two years earlier. She and her parents have retreated from each other and the world in their own ways. But a new neighbor who, Natalie learns, has survived her own terrible losses helps Natalie find the health and strength to begin living and reaching out again. Likable characters engage the reader in this credible, hopeful story.

♥ ***The Hope Tree: Kids Talk About Breast Cancer*** by Laura Joffe Numeroff and Wendy S. Harpham. Simon & Schuster, 2001. K–5. Numeroff and Harpham fictionalize real stories from children of breast cancer patients to give us insights into how the disease affects families. The children's observations address their feelings, fears, family interactions, adjustments and hopes.

♥ ***Jenny Archer to the Rescue*** by Ellen Conford. Little, Brown and Company, 1992. 2–4. Students may know Jenny Archer from other Conford books. In this story, Jenny is inspired by a newspaper article to become a hero by rescuing someone. She studies first aid but no one cooperates by needing her services! A fun, easy read.

♥ ***Mama One, Mama Two*** by Patricia MacLachlan. HarperCollins, 1982. K–3. Maudie and her foster mother share the story of how Maudie's mother became sad and depressed and Maudie came to live with her foster family. The sensitive story offers a glimpse into the impact of mental illness on families and the love, comfort and caring given by those who help.

♥ ***Officer Buckle and Gloria*** by Peggy Rathmann. Putnam, 1995. K–5. Caldecott Medal Book, ALA Notable Children's Book. Officer Buckle's mission is to share his infinite supply of safety tips with everyone in Napville. But he's boring so the school kids don't listen until Gloria, the new police dog, goes along. What will Officer Buckle do when he discovers his newfound popularity is really about Gloria stealing the show behind his back? This multiple award-winner is hilarious, delightful and full of safety tips.

♥ ***On My Honor*** by Marion Dane Bauer. Bantam Doubleday Dell, 1987. 3–5. Newbery Honor Book. In this intensely dramatic story, an adventure turns to sudden tragedy. Joel challenges his best friend Tony to swim to a sandbar in dangerous waters. Tony drowns, and Joel is left to deal with shock and guilt.

♥ ***Pig and the Shrink*** by Pamela Todd. Random House, 2000. 3–5. Runty, smart aleck Tucker needs a project for the junior high science fair fast. He convinces Angelo Pighetti, "Pig," to be his experimental subject in a project on nutrition and obesity. But as Tucker and Pig share experiences of dodging school bullies, creative weight-loss strategies and blossoming friendship they gain surprise insights all around. Funny, compelling characters draw the reader into a believable story of middle school angst and the search for belonging.

♥ ***Promises*** by Elizabeth Winthrop. Houghton Mifflin, 2000. K–3. Sarah deals with a range of emotions including fear, sadness, anger and embarrassment as her mother undergoes cancer treatment. This lovely picture book wraps the reader in the warmth of an honest, caring family of believable characters struggling with a difficult challenge.

♥ ***Stop Pretending: What Happened When My Big Sister Went Crazy*** by Sonya Sones. HarperCollins, 2001. 5+. Thirteen-year-old Cookie shares her experience of her sister's mental illness through poems. Her whirlwind of emotions is powerfully portrayed in this realistic, accessible and ultimately comforting novel. A moving, empathy building story for older readers.

♥ ***Swimmy*** by Leo Lionni. Knopf, 1991. K–3. Caldecott Honor Book. Swimmy learns the hard way that small fish can be victims in the big sea, losing all his playmates to a big, hungry tuna. His new playmates fear a similar fate. Swimmy saves the day when he shows them how to be safe by sticking together.

♥ ***A Wind in the Door*** by Madeleine L'Engle. Bantam Doubleday Dell, 2001. 4–5. This classic fantasy adventure sends Meg Murry on a terrifying race against time to save her seriously ill brother, and with him the balance of good and evil in the world, from a mysterious disease. The story addresses issues of schoolyard bullies, intolerance, courage and the healing power of love. L'Engle's masterful combination of irresistible characters, cosmic themes, fantastic creatures and heart-stopping action should appeal as much today as when originally published.

Nonfiction

♥ ***Disaster Blasters: A Kid's Guide to Being Home Alone*** by Karin Kasdin and Laura Szabo-Cohen. William Morrow & Co., 1996. 3–5. The authors use lots of humor and realistic scenarios to "de-borify" this safety guide for children who spend time at home without supervision. Kids from three fictional families find themselves in 21 safety crises and have to choose how to respond. The guide is packed with solid first aid and safety tips that address a wide range of real dangers. A great tool!

♥ ***Fit for Life*** by Alexandra Parsons. Grolier Publishing, 1996. 3–5. In this inviting little book, Parsons both introduces readers to the basics of child health (nutrition, exercise, hygiene and the dangers of substance abuse and eating disorders) and encourages them to take responsibility for their choices. Lively text, lots of colorful illustrations and comic book style vignettes entice readers to absorb the direct but lightly delivered messages. A good overview or starting place for research.

♥ ***Food and Your Health*** by Jillian Powell. Raintree Publishers, 1997. K–5. This Health Matters series title gives an overview of how the body works and what fuel it needs to function well. It covers basic food groups and nutrients and offers guidelines for a balanced diet. It is heavily illustrated, easy to read and packed with information—a good first stop. Other series titles: *Drugs and Your Health, Exercise and Your Health* and *Hygiene and Your Health.*

♥ ***Health Care*** by Deborah S. Romaine. Lucent Books, 1999. 4–5. Health care in the U.S. is examined in this Lucent Overview series volume. The book addresses availability of care, managed care, doctor shortages in rural areas, the aging population and the looming crisis of health care costs and Medicare. Especially interesting is information on the impact of smoking, obesity, teen pregnancy and other lifestyle choice issues in the country as a whole.

♥ ***Jonas Salk and the Polio Vaccine*** by John Bankston. Mitchell Lane Publishers, 2001. 4–5. Dr. Jonas Salk, son of Russian Jewish immigrants, helped eradicate polio with his inactivated vaccine. Along with Salk's brilliance and perseverance, the author stresses his humanitarian motives by noting his insistence on providing the medicine free of charge and forgoing the fortune he could have made by patenting the formula. Mention of animal testing throughout his research offers an interesting connection with the previous chapter. An Unlocking the Secrets of Science series title.

♥ ***Safety on the Internet*** by Lucia Raatma. Capstone Press, 1999. K–2. This easy-to-read book gives simple tips for safe and appropriate use of the Internet for children. It includes a glossary, full-page illustrations and lists of Web sites and search engines designed to be kid-safe and kid-friendly. A basic, practical tool. Other Safety First! series titles include *Safety around Fire, Safety around Strangers, Safety at Home* and *Safety on the School Bus.*

Other Media

♥ ***Fitness*** by Nordic Software. Nordic Software, 2000 (interactive CD). K–5. While not well packaged to attract kids, this program has lots of basic information and kid-friendly activities that reinforce good eating habits and exercise as contributors to fitness. A useful tool for students who like the interactive medium.

♥ ***The Graduation of Jake Moon*** by Barbara Park, narrated by Fred Savage. Listening Library Inc., 2000 (audiocassettes). 4–5. Jake Moon has lived with his mom and grandfather all his life. But when his grandfather gets Alzheimer's disease and Jake must increasingly play the role of caretaker, he struggles with resentment, anxiety and embarrassment. A funny, convincing and heartwarming story.

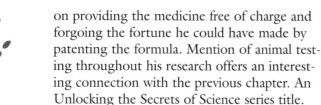

Web sites

♥ ***BBC Kids' Health***
www.bbc.co.uk/health/kids/

♥ ***FDA Kids' Homepage***
www.fda.gov/oc/opacom/kids/

♥ ***Healthfinder Kids***
www.healthfinder.gov/kids/

♥ ***Health & Human Services Pages for Kids***
www.hhs.gov/kids/

♥ ***KidsHealth***
www.kidshealth.org

♥ ***Think Quest "911 Safety Rage"***
library.thinkquest.org/J001802

Service-Learning in Action

Here are some examples of service-learning projects that involved elementary students working together to make their communities safer and healthier.

♥ **Child-Friendly Emergency Room, North Adams, Massachusetts**

Building on a partnership created several years ago between Roberta Sullivan's kindergarten class at Sullivan Elementary School in North Adams, Massachusetts, and the North Adams Regional Hospital, Sullivan's kindergartners recently created a kid-friendly space in the emergency room waiting area. They used math skills to measure the space and plan the layout. Creating a "Don't Be Afraid" book to comfort young visitors exercised language arts skills. They learned about science and health as they selected toys and other objects for the space that were safe and consistent with hospital goals. Decorating with quilts, murals and self-portraits gave students an outlet for artistic expression. Everybody won! Students are proud of themselves and their work and love to show off their accomplishments. And both young patients and hospital staff benefit from the welcoming, comforting atmosphere. Billie Ellard, Director of Emergency Nursing at the Hospital, reported that in the first months after opening the child-friendly waiting area, staff didn't have to use restraints to control agitated children even once! For more information contact:

Debbie Coyne
Service-Learning Coordinator
North Adams School District
413-662-3240
coyneds@hotmail.com

♥ **School Zone Traffic Safety, Pittsburgh, Pennsylvania**

Second-graders at Woolslair Elementary School in Pittsburgh, Pennsylvania, made conditions safer for their entire school community. Suspecting traffic hazards in front of the school, they tallied traffic and counted pedestrian violations on the street. Partnering with a city councilman and the League of Women Voters, they organized a poster march around the school urging drivers to slow down. They also convinced the City Council to place a guardrail along the front of the school. Jaywalking has stopped and drivers show more caution as they pass through the school zone. As a follow-up to their efforts, students met with the City Council, visited the mayor's office and appeared on the city's cable TV program. Athene Hopkins, one of the lead teachers on the project, can provide more information. Contact Athene Hopkins at:

Woolslair Elementary School
501 40th Street
Pittsburgh, PA 15224
412-623-8800
athenehopkins@cs.com

Discussion Prompts

Use the following prompts to explore issues of health and safety.

♥ **Safety in Numbers.** Read *Swimmy* as a class. Discuss Swimmy's idea for achieving safety in numbers and brainstorm ways that "sticking together" can help students stay safe.

♥ **Exploring Mental Illness.** Review *Anna and the Cat Lady,* focusing on the end of Chapter 6 where Anna reflects on her feelings about Mrs. Sarafiny's strange behavior and what she might do to help.

- Describe Mrs. Sarafiny. Why do the girls like her in spite of her odd behavior? What behaviors make the girls worry about her?

- Why does mental illness make us feel uncomfortable? Why do we feel fear when people don't behave as we expect them to?

- When should we feel obligated to do something to help someone who is mentally ill?

- What do the girls do to help Mrs. Sarafiny? What might you do to help someone suffering from mental illness that would be safe for you and respectful of your friend?

♥ **Round Robin Reading.** Divide older students into four groups. Assign group 1 to read *On My Honor,* group 2 *Flapjack Waltzes,* group 3 *A Wind in the Door* and group 4 *Diving for the Moon.* Encourage students to read carefully, paying special attention to issues related to physical and emotional health and safety. After reading, group students according to the plan below and have the combined groups discuss the issues indicated. Each paired discussion group should take a minute to summarize the plots of their respective books and to choose a reporter to take notes so a brief summary can be given to the rest of the class after the discussions. Discussions may be brief—perhaps 15 minutes per grouping. This "round robin" format allows students to come away with a broad synthesis of ideas on the subject.

- Groups 1 and 2 should discuss the feelings of the main characters after the deaths in the books. What was the strongest emotion for each? Both main characters try to pull back from other people and avoid dealing with their painful feelings. How do they do this? Are they successful? Does their isolation help them in any way? What draws them back into the world to face and deal with their feelings? Do you think they are better off after they reconnect with people? Why or why not?

- At the same time, groups 3 and 4 should compare and contrast the "best friendships" in the two books—between Bird and Josh in *Diving for the Moon* and Calvin and Meg in *A Wind in the Door.* How are these friendships similar and different? How do these best friends try to protect each other's physical health and safety? How do they support each other to have healthy emotions and attitudes? How can you and your friends help each other be safe and healthy?

- Now rearrange groups. Groups 2 and 3 should discuss the relationships between the main characters and their brothers in the books. While Natalie's brother, in *Flapjack Waltzes,* was older and is dead at the time of the story and Meg's brother, in *A Wind in the Door,* is younger and ill, both books reveal the relationships. How are they similar and different? Do they seem like normal sibling relationships? How do you think you'd feel if your brother or sister's health or life were threatened? Do siblings have a special responsibility to try to protect each other? What do you think Natalie and Meg might say to each other if they met?

- At the same time, groups 1 and 4 should discuss the impact on the main characters of the threat to a best friend. In *On My Honor,* Joel's best friend dies in a tragic accident. In *Diving for the Moon,* Bird's best friend's life is threatened by HIV/AIDS. While one story has a happy (for now) ending and the other does not, how are the experiences of the main characters similar? Both main characters deal with feelings of responsibility for and dependence on their best friends. What does each main character learn and how does he or she grow from the experiences? How do you think you might feel if your best friend became very ill or died? Do you think best friends have a special responsibility to try to protect each other? How can best friends help each other be safe and healthy?

- Regroup one last time. Groups 1 and 3 should discuss caution and courage in their books' main characters. Meg in *A Wind in the Door* and Joel in *On My Honor* are both cautious people by nature. Yet they both find courage to act when someone they love is in danger. What courageous things do these characters do in the books? What motivates them to overcome their cautious natures? What do you think each learns about himself or herself? What role does caution play in staying healthy and safe? What role does courage play?

- Groups 2 and 4 should discuss their main characters' common experiences of anger after the crises in their lives. At whom is the anger directed? Does the anger "make sense?" How does each character express or cope with anger? Natalie, in *Flapjack Waltzes*, has had some time to come to terms with her anger. What advice do you think she might give Bird about dealing with her anger and fear of loss?

♥ **Expressing Emotions.** In several of the books (e.g., *Promises, Flapjack Waltzes)*, pressures and losses cause characters to hide their emotions or express them in ways that are unhealthy. Identify several common emotions (anger, sadness, happiness, fear, etc.). Write them on a board or flipchart. Invite students to suggest healthy, safe, appropriate ways to express those emotions. For example, under the word "anger," you might come up with running around the block, beating up your pillow, talking to a trusted adult or drawing an angry picture. You might copy your completed lists for students to use on their own as they deal with emotions in their everyday lives.

Games

♥ **Anagram Game.** Anagrams are words made up of letters found in another word, used as the source word. See how many words you can find using any combination of the letters in the source words "Health and Safety."

♥ **Health and Safety Photo Scavenger Hunt.** Divide the class into four teams. Give each team a Polaroid camera loaded with film and a copy of a tasks and points list like the one on page 37. You may copy and use the list as it is or adapt it to suit your particular school situation. Set a time limit (perhaps one class period), notify students that they are not to disturb classes in progress or to leave school property and send the teams off to find and shoot as many of the assigned pictures as they can. You may wish to send an adult volunteer with each team for safety's sake. At the appointed time collect the team photos, tally the points (you might subtract points from teams returning late) and announce the winners.

Creative Expressions

Enjoy these creative ways to process concepts from the chapter's books.

♥ **Role-Playing—Dares and Challenges.** Review either *Arnie and the Skateboard Gang* or *On My Honor*, as appropriate for your class. Talk about the challenge or dare to do something dangerous in the story and how the challenged character responds. Then divide the class into teams of 2–4 students. Each team will make up a scenario in which children challenge or dare each other to do something dangerous. They will role-play two responses to the challenge: first, what might happen if the dare is accepted, and second, how the child might refuse the challenge in order to protect himself.

♥ **Poetry Writing.** Invite interested students to read *Stop Pretending: What Happened When My Big Sister Went Crazy* and to try their hands at writing free verse poems expressing the emotions of difficult times in their lives.

♥ **Eating for Health.** Have students create menus for healthy, balanced meals, including recipes. You might have the class vote on their favorite menus and try cooking them together, using the school kitchen or a home economics classroom. Students might start by reviewing *Fit for Life* or *Food and Your Health* or do an Internet search using search terms like "nutrition" or "healthy recipes."

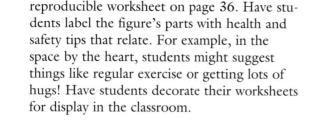

♥ **Health and Safety Tips.** Hand out the reproducible worksheet on page 36. Have students label the figure's parts with health and safety tips that relate. For example, in the space by the heart, students might suggest things like regular exercise or getting lots of hugs! Have students decorate their worksheets for display in the classroom.

Research Opportunities

♥ **Health Hazards.** Assign each student to research one potential health or safety hazard and become an amateur expert on its prevention and handling. To add a creative component, have students express their findings by writing challenges about their hazard similar to those in *Disaster Blasters.*

♥ **Safety Sleuths.** Accompany the class, together or in teams, as they tour the school and school grounds looking for possible health or safety hazards. Document your findings with photos and careful notes about what, where and the dangers posed. Based on your findings, prepare a "Safety Report Card" to present to the principal, including your overall assessment of the school's safety, your specific findings and suggestions for removing hazards.

♥ **Health and Safety Heroes.** Review *Jonas Salk and the Polio Vaccine*. Invite students to identify a Health and Safety Hero—either a historical figure or someone living today—whose efforts have made the world healthier and safer for them. Have them study that person and write a one-page biographical sketch to share with the class.

Miscellaneous Activities

♥ **School Lunches.** Meet with your school nutritionist to discuss school lunches. Find out how lunch menus are planned, ask questions about good nutrition and discuss ways to improve menus to be more nutritious and appealing to students.

♥ **Help for Latchkey Kids.** Find out what safe after-school programs exist in your community for children with working parents. Create and distribute a flyer to get the word out.

In Your Community

Use these starting points to discover needs and activity in your local community.

♥ Look in the phone book. Check the yellow pages under headings like "Health Care," "Health, Fitness & Nutrition," "Safety," "Mental Health Services," "First Aid" and "Nutritionists." Some specific health problems are also listed, like "Alcoholism—Information & Treatment" or "Eating Disorders—Information & Treatment." Check government pages under "Health and Human Services," "Public Health," "Public Safety," "Fire" or "Police."

♥ Call your city hall or county supervisor's office and ask what government services promote health and safety, and what organizations in the community work to help them.

♥ Check out SERVEnet (www.servenet.org) to see what organizations that deal with health and safety issues are listed for your area.

♥ Watch the local newspapers and other publications for articles on health and safety.

♥ Talk to people "in the know." They might be government employees like the police chief or fire chief, or directors of community service facilities like hospitals. Invite such resource people to visit the class or assign students to interview appropriate people and report back. Learn what these people feel are the greatest needs in the local community.
Note: Don't overlook the school community! Your principal, counselor, nutritionist, nurse or other school staff may have ideas of health or safety needs within the school district that could use some attention.

Taking Action

Based on your exploration of health and safety challenges, plan your service-learning project. These ideas might spark suggestions.

♥ Build on your work from Research Opportunities on page 34 to create a safety newsletter for your school. You might feature one safety issue (stranger danger, fire safety, gun safety, household poisons, etc.) per issue or include regular columns on common issues.

♥ Does your school have a problem with bullies? Set up a "Safe Escort" service made up of student teams who see potential victims safely to and from school.

♥ Start an anti-smoking or anti-drug campaign in your school. Consider working with the local police department's D.A.R.E. program.

♥ Depending on the specific needs in your community, work with your PTA or PTO to educate kids and parents about the importance of regular medical or dental check-ups or immunizations for kids. You might sponsor a free immunization clinic, partnering with local health care providers.

♥ Survey students to identify what diseases have touched their lives most (cancer? alcoholism? AIDS? Alzheimer's?), then make a plan to raise awareness and funds to fight that disease.

♥ Write skits to perform at an assembly that demonstrate home-alone safety scenarios and tips.

♥ Find out what should be included in first aid/emergency kits. Then design the kits, raise funds for the materials, assemble the kits and present them to each classroom in the school.

♥ Sponsor a First Aid/CPR training class for your whole school, in partnership with a local Red Cross chapter or other agency.

More Ideas

Share these ideas with motivated students who want to help as individuals.

♥ Keep yourself fit and healthy through good nutrition, hygiene and exercise.

♥ Start a fitness or safety club with your friends.

♥ Refuse to accept dangerous challenges or dares and encourage your peers to do the same.

♥ Talk to your parents about volunteering to visit patients at a local hospital.

♥ Participate in fundraisers in support of local organizations that promote public health and safety.

♥ Keep learning about the issues and expressing your informed views to your local paper, local government officials and national politicians.

Health and Safety Tips Worksheet

Label the figure's parts with related health and safety tips. An example has been done for you. If you have time, decorate your worksheets for display in the classroom.

Head

Nose

Eyes

Mouth

Hands and Arms

Heart
Get lots of exercise.
Get lots of hugs!

Stomach

Legs and Feet

Health and Safety
Photo Scavenger Hunt

Your team's challenge is to bring back photos of items or activities from the list below. Your teacher will tell you how long you have to plan your strategy, take your photos and return. All photos must be taken on school property. No team may submit more than 10 photos. The team with the most points wins! Check off photos as you take them.

Good luck! Have fun! Be courteous!

_____ One or more team members identifying an unmarked potential health or safety hazard in the building or on school grounds. *(2 points)*

_____ The place you go in your school when you don't feel well. *(2 points. One extra point if you get a photo of the school nurse or other staff member taking a team member's temperature!)*

_____ A piece of safety equipment somewhere in the school, such as a smoke alarm, fire alarm, first aid kit, etc. *(2 points)*

_____ Two or more team members demonstrating safe use of a piece of sports equipment. *(2 points)*

_____ A team member demonstrating proper hand washing after restroom use. *(2 points)*

_____ A sign or message posted in the school warning of a possible danger. *(2 points)*

_____ A sign or message posted in the school that promotes a safe or healthy habit. *(2 points. Two extra points if the team makes up such a sign or message and gets permission to post it.)*

_____ Two or more team members acting out (SAFELY!) an accident that might happen at school. *(2 points)*

_____ One or more team members demonstrating an activity that might protect their emotional or mental health. Be creative! *(Up to 2 points.)*

_____ A creative photo showing all team members doing something to make the school building or grounds safer for students and staff. *(Up to 5 additional points.)*

The Natural Environment

We all know that clean water and air and a healthy planet are critical to our own well-being, even to our survival. Many of us appreciate the emotional and spiritual refreshment we take from the beauty of the natural world. The idea of taking care of the environment is so obvious and appealing that it would be hard to find anyone to oppose it. Hence the success of so-called "green" movements and consumer products. On the other hand, we are a nation that lives in the moment and expects a material lifestyle that places excessive demands on the resources and protective systems of the earth. How much we let concern for the environment impact our daily actions varies widely. As a nation we continue to consume far more than our share and support our lifestyle habits in ways that damage and endanger the earth.

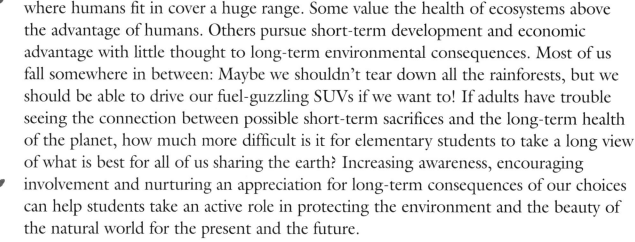

As with our attitudes toward animal welfare, our ideas about the natural world and where humans fit in cover a huge range. Some value the health of ecosystems above the advantage of humans. Others pursue short-term development and economic advantage with little thought to long-term environmental consequences. Most of us fall somewhere in between: Maybe we shouldn't tear down all the rainforests, but we should be able to drive our fuel-guzzling SUVs if we want to! If adults have trouble seeing the connection between possible short-term sacrifices and the long-term health of the planet, how much more difficult is it for elementary students to take a long view of what is best for all of us sharing the earth? Increasing awareness, encouraging involvement and nurturing an appreciation for long-term consequences of our choices can help students take an active role in protecting the environment and the beauty of the natural world for the present and the future.

There is a wealth of picture books extolling the beauty and importance of nature. The same is true for nonfiction books and series exploring ecosystems and environmental issues. (See the Geography Detective and the Earth Watch series from Carolrhoda Books, Ecosystems of North America from Benchmark Books, Restoring Nature: Success Stories from Children's Press and other series represented in the bibliography.) However, there is a shortage of solid fiction for children that is not set in a fantasy, horror, time travel or other "removed from reality" context. Does this reflect our culture's ambivalent attitude toward environmental issues? Perhaps it's easy for us to love the beauty of nature, but hard to face the here-and-now responsibilities of our daily lifestyle choices.

What are the issues of environmental health in your community, and how can you address them? These topics might help focus your exploration of the environment.

- ♥ Importance of respecting the balance of nature.

- ♥ The world's major ecosystems.

- ♥ Being good stewards of the earth's resources.

- ♥ What happens to the waste we discard?

- ♥ Our air and water—How clean are they?

- ♥ Fostering a long-term perspective on protecting our environment.

- ♥ How opportunities to enjoy the beauty of nature benefit us.

- ♥ Balancing the need for economic development with protecting the environment.

Resources on the Natural Environment

Use these resources to build knowledge of the natural environment.

Fiction

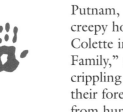

The Beasties by William Sleator. Penguin Putnam, 1999. 4–5+. This compellingly creepy horror story pulls Doug and his sister Colette into the terrifying world of "The Family," a subterranean race that survives the crippling effects of inbreeding and attacks on their forest habitat by stealing body parts from humans. Not for the squeamish, but for lovers of the horror genre this is an effective look at the implications of our destruction of habitats in the name of development.

City Green by DyAnne DiSalvo-Ryan. William Morrow & Co., 1994. K–5. When an old building is razed in her urban neighborhood, Marcy and her friend Miss Rosa turn the lot into a community garden. In the process they create an oasis of beauty, make friends and bring people together. An endnote gives instructions for starting a community garden.

Creature Crossing by Betty Levin. Greenwillow Books, 1999. 3–5. Ben is disappointed when the strange creature he finds turns out to be a salamander, rather than the dinosaur embryo he had imagined would bring him fame and fortune. But his friends Kate and Foster, and the whole neighborhood, rally behind an effort to divert traffic and save the endangered salamanders from mass slaughter as they cross the road on their annual migration back to their breeding pools. A quick, satisfying read about characters learning to care more for their fellow creatures than for their own short-term pleasure.

Earthdance by Joanne Ryder. Henry Holt & Company, 1999. K–5. This breathtaking picture book invites children to identify with, appreciate and celebrate the earth. Its irresistible message is respect for our shared home and all living things on it. An excellent read-aloud introduction or conclusion to a unit of study on caring for the earth.

Green Boy by Susan Cooper. Margaret K. McElderry Books, 2002. 4–5. Twelve-year-old Trey and his mute 7-year-old brother Lou find themselves at the center of an ancient

battle between the forces of greedy development and lovers of the natural world, in a plot parallel to their "real" battle to save their favorite Bahamian island from present-day developers. The environmental message is blatant but dramatic in this exciting fantasy.

Hoot by Carl Hiaasen. Random House, 2002. 5+. Newbery Honor Book. Hiaasen pits Roy Eberhardt, a middle schooler whose family moves a lot, against a classic bully and a bunch of greedy corporate types determined to build their restaurant on land that houses a protected owl species. Roy is believable and endearing as a reluctant hero whose main goal is to survive the challenges of always being "the new kid." Wonderful, quirky characters, crisp writing, sometimes dark humor and a satisfying resolution make this a "must read."

Just a Dream by Chris Van Allsburg. Houghton Mifflin, 1990. K–5. After a night of dreams showing the future of an Earth ruined by man's thoughtlessness, Walter changes his attitude towards environmental awareness in the present. Van Allsburg's evocative illustrations make this a rewarding, if sharply pointed, picture book experience.

The Missing 'Gator of Gumbo Limbo by Jean Craighead George. HarperCollins, 1993. 3–5. Liza K. and the other "woods people," who live in a rare and forgotten area of the Everglades, panic when a contract hunter comes to kill the oversized alligator who keeps intruders away. The group of homeless nature lovers pull together to try to find and save the 'gator and, in solving the mystery of his whereabouts, accomplish surprising victories for each of them and their beloved ecosystem. An information-packed page-turner.

Mr. Garbage by William H. Hooks. Gareth Stevens Publishing, 1996. K–4. This Bank Street series reader follows Eli as his enthusiasm for recycling causes him to go overboard on a recycling adventure starting in his own room and extending throughout the neighborhood. A humorous look at how garbage accumulates and what happens to it.

The Salamander Room by Anne Mazer. Knopf, 1994. K–3. In this richly illustrated picture book, Brian finds a salamander in the woods and brings it home. His mother helps him imagine how he will provide for its needs, until he has created a fantasy habitat in his bedroom. A front note invites students to become "habitat detectives," carefully observing the elements that make up a habitat.

♥ ***Someday a Tree*** by Eve Bunting. Houghton Mifflin, 1996. K–3. Bunting features a community trying to save the life of a beloved old tree poisoned by dumped chemicals. Ronald Himler's comforting illustrations soften the impact of the emotional, pointed text about specific consequences of pollution. A good starting point for discussion.

♥ ***What Planet Are You From, Clarice Bean?*** by Lauren Child. Candlewick Press, 2002. K–5. The irrepressible Clarice Bean is back, complete with wacky illustrations, "from the mouths of babes" dialogue and delightfully chaotic layout. This time Clarice opts to join her family as an ecowarrior, saving an old neighborhood tree from being chopped down, rather than tackle the boring project assigned by her sour-as-lemons teacher. A delightful romp that invites giggles and discussion.

♥ ***Wild in the City*** by Jan Thornhill. Maple Tree Press, 1999. K–5. Jenny hears a noise outside her window at night. As she falls asleep the wild night creatures in the neighborhood swing into action. This picture book explores the lives and relationships of wild animals in the city. A delightful invitation to look closer at the natural world around us.

♥ ***Window*** by Jeannie Baker. HarperCollins, 1991. K–5. In this wordless picture book we look through a bedroom window at the view as a young boy grows up. During the 20+ years, the scene changes from pristine countryside to congested, paved-over city. In the last spread the boy—now a man with his own son—looks out another window at a lush, rural view compromised by a developer's sign across the river. Breathtaking collages provide rich detail and make the book's message about how quickly we are destroying wild places clear. A wonderful discussion-starter.

Nonfiction

♥ ***American Environmental Heroes*** by Phyllis M. Stanley. Enslow Publishers, 1996. 4–5. This eye-opening title in Enslow's Collective Biography series offers introductions to several aspects of environmental awareness through its concise biographies of ten environmentalists. Students may be inspired by the impressive work of the likes of Ellen Swallow Richards, George Washington Carver, Aldo Leopold and Frances Moore Lappe, as they learn of the conviction which each of these activists brings to his or her belief in the interconnectedness of all living things on the planet. Supplemental information on national parks by state.

♥ ***Brother Eagle, Sister Sky*** by Chief Seattle. Penguin Putnam, 2002. K–5. In Chief Seattle's response to the U.S. government's request to buy the lands of the Northwest Nations, he eloquently sets forth Native American respect for the sacredness of the land and all life on it. He calls us to share and carry on that respect. A veritable manifesto for the environmental movement.

♥ ***Common Ground: The Water, Earth, and Air We Share*** by Molly Bang. Scholastic, 1997. 1–5. Bang presents a simple fable about a community that overgrazed its "commons" to the detriment of all, followed by a series of analogous situations in our world today. A bright, accessible little book that invites discussion and stimulates reflection on taking a long view of the consequences of our actions.

♥ ***Eco-fun*** by David Suzuki. Douglas & McIntyre Publications, 2001. 3–5. Suzuki offers 48 activities designed to help children learn about the environment. Chapters dealing with air, water, the Earth, the sun's power and plants and animals organize the activities, which are mostly traditional science experiments punctuated with games and offbeat options like "Animal Yoga." Drawings help illustrate easy-to-follow directions and Suzuki's chatty enthusiasm should entice even resistant students.

♥ ***Global Warming: The Threat of Earth's Changing Climate*** by Laurence Pringle. SeaStar Books, 2001. 4–5. Dramatic photos and clear, balanced text set forth what we know and don't know about global warming and climate change. Acknowledging that we can't be sure how much of the change in Earth's climate is due to humans, it still makes a powerful case for acting now to reduce the greenhouse gases and move to cleaner energy sources.

♥ ***A Handful of Dirt*** by Raymond Bial. Walker & Company, 2000. K–5. Have you ever really thought about a handful of dirt? This fascinating picture book explores the microscopic mysteries of life and process, energy potential and transfer going on all the time in the soil beneath

our feet. Great photos and directions for creating compost round out this excellent title.

♥ **Nuclear Power** by Ian Graham. Raintree Publishers, 1999. 3–5. This enthralling title in the Energy Forever? series makes the complex subject of the science and dangers of nuclear power comprehensible. Lots of photos, drawings and sidebars support the well-written text. The series also addresses wind, solar, water, geothermal and bio-energy sources.

♥ **Pass the Energy, Please!** by Barbara Shaw McKinney. Dawn Publications, 2000. K–5. From the meadow, ocean, plains, woodlands and Arctic tundra McKinney introduces the concept of "passing the energy" through food chains in the natural world. The thoughtful poem inspires wonder as well as respect for nature's cycles of energy transfer.

♥ **Pond** by Donald M. Silver. McGraw-Hill Professional, 1997. 1–5. This One Small Square series title uses clear, detailed text and extraordinary art to guide a careful adventure of discovery of pond life. Sidebars, science experiments and drawings of microscopic life engage the reader and elicit wonder at this complex ecosystem. The book can be used to explore a real pond or as a self-contained experience. Other series titles explore the seashore, a cave, an arctic tundra, etc.

♥ **A River Ran Wild: An Environmental History** by Lynne Cherry. Harcourt Brace Jovanovich, 2002. 1–5. This lovely historical picture book tells of the Nashua River from nearly 7,000 years ago until the early '90s, focusing on the environmental issues of use, abuse, pollution and clean-up. It gently features the dedicated, persistent efforts of Marion Stoddart to clean up the river and restore its healthy purity.

♥ **Up River** by Frank Asch. Simon & Schuster, 1995. 2–5. Asch shares his son's experience on an annual canoe brigade to clean up garbage in Otter Creek through lively text and sparkling photos. A cheerful and informative book that might inspire similar efforts.

♥ **Wildfires** by Seymour Simon. HarperCollins, 2000. 3–5. This striking picture book with full-page photos demonstrates both the destructive and the regenerating power of naturally occurring fires on burned habitats. Simon comments on lessons we have learned about wildlife management through our mistakes in handling wildfires. Beautiful and balanced.

♥ **The World's Wild Places** by John Howson. Raintree Publishers, 1998. 4–5. Wild places and growing threats to them are explored in this Protecting Our Planet series title. Expectations of higher standards of living and corresponding increases in waste products speed up the destruction. Colorful photos; useful maps of the world's mountains, wetlands, forests, etc.; and clever, engaging text offer an excellent overview. Lots of recommended resources increase research value.

Other Media

♥ **Evergreen, Everblue** by Raffi. Rounder/ PGD, 1996 (CD). K–3. Raffi sings lovely, fun songs about respecting and caring for the earth. Old favorites like "One Light, One Sun" join forces with message songs like "Clean Rain" and "Big Beautiful Planet." Great for background music or to stimulate creative expression.

♥ **The Magic Schoolbus: Getting Energized** by Joanna Cole. Scholastic, 1997 (videocassette). K–5. Ms. Frizzle takes kids on another Magic Schoolbus adventure to find alternative ways to run a carnival Ferris wheel when the electricity fails and their fundraiser is threatened. The kids learn about wind, water and solar power as they assemble an ingenious system to turn the Ferris wheel. A conversation with the fictional producer of the TV series deals with some of the safety and credibility issues that might make adults nervous.

Web sites

♥ **Carly's Kids Corner**
www.treecityusa.org/carly

♥ **Earth Day on Your Block**
www.allspecies.org/neigh/block.htm

♥ **Envirofun (Illinois EPA)**
www.epa.state.il.us/kids/

♥ **Rainforest Alliance**
www.rainforest-alliance.org/kids&teachers

♥ **Ranger Rick's Kidzone**
www.nwf.org/kids

♥ **U.S. EPA Explorer's Club**
www.epa.gov/kids
An interesting page on Garbage & Recycling, along with other information.

Service-Learning in Action

Here are some examples of service-learning projects in which elementary school students worked to keep the environment healthy for us all.

♥ **Hoosic River Watershed Exploration, North Adams, Massachusetts**

During May of 2002, fifth graders from Sullivan Elementary School in North Adams, Massachusetts, completed a project sponsored by the North Adams Parks and Recreation Department and the Hoosic River Watershed Association. Students visited Windsor Lake, part of the Hoosic River Watershed. They collected and studied water samples from both natural and man-manipulated parts of the lake to identify organisms and analyze the health of the lake. Naturalist Kimberly Jensen helped students explore relevant food chains. Based on their studies and using natural objects, students created works of art depicting food chains under the direction of local artist Ann Kremers. The individual chains were linked to demonstrate the interconnectedness of life in the watershed. The finished product was displayed at Hoosic River's annual Riverfest to raise public awareness of the complexity and importance of the watershed. Other hands-on activities and classroom follow-ups gave students creative and research opportunities to consolidate their learning. Teamwork flourished and excitement was high; students enjoyed explaining their work to others. Classroom teachers on the project were Cindy Grosso, Kathy Atwood and Jeanne Dorsky. For more information, contact:

Debbie Coyne
Service-Learning Coordinator
North Adams School District
413-662-3240
coyneds@hotmail.com

♥ **Prairie Restoration, Council Bluffs, Iowa**

Another summer school project involved about 30 K–12 students from Council Bluffs, Iowa, in prairie restoration. With funding provided by an Action Research Grant during the summer of 1998, students embarked on the Loess Hills Ecology and Preservation project offered by the Council Bluffs Community Schools. Combined with study of prairie ecology under the direction of Summer Institute Team Leader Jan Pearson, Susanne Hickey of the Loess Hills Preservation Society identified an overgrown remnant of prairie in a large cemetery for the group to cut and reclaim. This proved to be hard, but rewarding, physical labor! Students further explored natural prairie objects and expressed newfound knowledge creatively as they made spirit pouches and pencil holders. They were enthusiastic and proud of their efforts. The Franklin Elementary School Ecology Club, advised by Jan Pearson (now Faraci), continues to maintain the prairie remnant with twice-yearly cuttings. To learn more about this project contact:

Jan Faraci
jfaraci@cbcsd.org

Activities on the Natural Environment

Discussion Prompts

Use these prompts to stimulate discussion of environmental issues.

♥ **Terrific Trees!** Draw a tree, bare of leaves, on the board. Review *Someday a Tree* and/or *What Planet Are You From, Clarice Bean?* with students and point out that in each of these books people go to great lengths to save one particular tree. Then ask, "What's special about a tree? What is a tree good for? What does it provide?" As students suggest answers ("It makes oxygen," "It can hold a swing," "It makes food for squirrels," etc.) add a leaf to the tree with a student response written on it. Encourage students to keep brainstorming until you have many leaves on the tree.

♥ **Booktalks and Discussion.** Assign older readers to one of two groups. One group will read *Green Boy* and the other *The Beasties*. After reading their books each group should meet to create a two-minute booktalk designed to entice the rest of the class to read their book, and choose an expressive speaker to present the talk. Explain that rather than summarizing the book and explaining theme and style, as in traditional book reports, book-talks should be brief and exciting. Students might use short passages from the text or "teasers" to grab attention and spark curiosity. After the presentations, lead the class in a discussion of the books using these prompts:

• What is the main issue in each book?

• Summarize the conflict between economic development and environmental protection in each book.

• Both authors use sibling teams as the main characters. Why do you think they do this?

• Both books are fantasies—readers are not asked to accept these stories as "real." There are many stories about environmental issues written in the form of fantasies (futuristic, time-travel, horror, etc.) and not many written as realistic contemporary children's novels. Why do you think so many authors interested in writing about environmental issues choose to write fantasies rather than realistic novels?

• What new ideas about the relationships between people and nature did you take from the story?

♥ **Debates.** Assign individuals or teams to debate affirmative and negative environmental resolutions. They will research their topics (*Global Warming, Nuclear Power, Wildfires* or *The World's Wild Places* are good starting points), then present arguments and rebuttals. The class might vote by show of hands to determine which side was more convincing. These ideas will get you started. Add your own or let students suggest other resolutions.

• All use of atomic energy (in weapons or power generation) should be banned as unsafe.

• The United States should change its position and support the Kyoto Protocol to reduce greenhouse gases.

• Wild places should be preserved, no matter what short-term economic advantages their development might provide.

• Naturally occurring wildfires should be allowed to burn themselves out.

Games

♥ **Wordsearch.** Enjoy the wordsearch puzzle on the handout on page 47, using words and phrases that relate to nature and the environment. You might provide a word bank for younger students.

♥ **Environmental Slogan Game.** Write the word "Ecosystem" on the board vertically. Divide the class into four teams and give each team nine 4" x 6" index cards and colored markers. Teams will work together to create slogans reflecting support for some aspect of environmental protection—one starting with each letter in the word "ecosystem." For example, the "y" card might read, "YES to Recycling!" The team that completes slogans for all nine letters first wins. When each team has finished, have the class arrange the index cards on paper or poster board to create a classroom collage of slogans and decorate it with appropriate drawings and symbols.

Creative Expressions

Enjoy these creative ways to process concepts from the books on the list.

♥ **Fantastic Drawings.** Both *Just a Dream* and *The Salamander Room* share dreamlike fantasies about environmental issues. Review these books with the class. Then invite students to complete one of these assignments:

- Choose an animal, like the salamander in *The Salamander Room,* and draw a picture of how you might create a fantasy habitat for that animal in your room.

- Choose a particular danger to the environment and draw a fantasy picture warning people about how the future might look if that danger is not addressed now.

♥ **Creating Fables or Parables.** Read *Common Ground* aloud and/or review *Window.* Talk about how the books show that changes to the environment happen gradually—decisions we make today may not change our lives drastically right now, but may damage the earth for our children and grandchildren. Invite students to write their own fables or parables warning readers about the consequences of today's treatment of the environment for future generations.

♥ **Celebrating Mother Earth!** Share *Earthdance* and *Brother Eagle, Sister Sky* as read-aloud group experiences or at a learning center, along with *Evergreen, Everblue.* Then invite students to create a poem, song or dance celebrating our relationship to the earth and all the living things on it. Have students share their creations with the class.

Research Opportunities

♥ **Recycling Garbage.** Look at *Mr. Garbage* as a class. Then use the reproducible handout on page 48 to create a chart of common consumer products that we use and throw away, what happens to them and how they might be reused or recycled. An example is done for you on the chart. Arrange for students to use classroom and media center resources to complete the chart. The Recycle City Web site (www.epa.gov/recyclecity) is a great resource.

♥ **Environmental Organizations.** Have students research several environmental organizations and compare and contrast their history, beliefs, goals and methods. Some organiza-

tions to study might be the Sierra Club, Greenpeace, the National Arbor Day Foundation, the Rainforest Alliance, the National Wildlife Federation, the National Audubon Society, Nature Conservancy and Earthfirst! After hearing about the organizations, ask students which they would like to join and why.

♥ **Champions of the Earth.** Have students study historical or contemporary American environmental activists. *American Environmental Heroes* and *A River Ran Wild* are good starting points. Then invite nominations for a Class Environmental Hero. Students should support their nominations with brief descriptions of their candidates' accomplishments. Have the class vote by show of hands.

♥ **Ecosystems.** Assign students to research one of the planet's major ecosystems (wetlands, rainforests, etc.) and make posters displaying the main characteristics, plants, animals and food chains in that system to share with the class.

♥ **Food Chains.** Using *Pass the Energy, Please!* or the Planetpals food chain Web site (www.planetpals.com/foodchain.html) as a model, research and create a visual representation of a food chain that operates as part of an ecosystem in your local community.

Miscellaneous Activities

♥ **Conservation Inventory.** Have students keep lists of choices they make in a single day that impact the environment—what products they buy, how they use energy or water, what they discard, how their families clean their homes or manage their gardens, etc. Then, based on their first lists, have them create second lists of tips for more earth-friendly habits they can practice every day. *Eco-fun* includes a "Green Home Quiz" that might be used here, as might the National Wildlife Federation's Green Home Web site (nationalwildlife.org/backyardwildlifehabitat/greenhome.cfm).

♥ **Nature Hike.** Take the class on a nature walk in a nearby park or wild place. If possible, have a knowledgeable guide lead the walk and share information about the plants and animals that live there. Discuss both what we can learn about the natural world and how time spent in nature makes us feel.

♥ **Field Trip.** Arrange to visit a community garden, botanical center or garden club. Ask someone at the facility to explain what they do to help protect the environment.

Protecting Our Environment Right Here

In Your Community

Use these starting points to discover needs and activity in your local community.

- ♥ Check out the phone book. Look in the yellow pages under headings like "Environmental & Ecological Organizations, "Agricultural Consultants," "Garden Centers," "Recycling" or "Waste Removal—Hazardous." Under government listings, try "Parks & Recreation," "Public Works," "Department of Agriculture" or "Department of Natural Resources."

- ♥ Call your city hall or county supervisor's office and ask what agencies work with environmental issues and what community organizations help.

- ♥ Check out SERVEnet (www.servenet.org) to see what organizations are addressing these issues in your area.

- ♥ Watch local newspapers and other publications for articles on how people work to make communities more aware of the need to protect nature.

- ♥ Talk to people "in the know" on this subject. They might be government employees or members of nonprofit organizations like the Sierra Club or the National Arbor Day Foundation. You might invite these resource people to visit the class or assign students to practice communication, research and presentation skills by interviewing them and reporting back. Find out what these people see as the greatest challenges to having an ecologically healthy community.

Taking Action

Based on your research about environmental issues in your community, plan a service-learning project. These ideas might help you start generating suggestions.

- ♥ Sponsor a tree-planting project on school grounds or at a local park.

- ♥ Plant a garden on school grounds and use organic methods to control weeds and insects.

Choose plants that will attract local birds or butterflies. Include houses for bats or birds. Look into having your project certified as part of the Schoolyard Habitats program of the National Wildlife Federation (national-wildlife.org/schoolyardhabitats).

- ♥ Conduct an energy audit or a waste materials audit at your school and discuss your findings with the principal. Work with school administrators to develop plans to conserve energy or cut down waste by reducing, reusing and recycling. Consider challenging another school to compete with you in a conservation contest.

- ♥ Start a school Environmental Club to study community issues, raise awareness and tackle local environmental problems

- ♥ Based on your individual conservation inventories and idea lists, create skits and a take-home resource about making earth-friendly daily choices. Perform the skits and distribute the handouts at a school assembly.

- ♥ Arrange with a local environmental agency to volunteer for a clean-up project at a local park or river.

More Ideas

Offer these ideas to motivated students who want to help as individuals.

- ♥ Ask your parents to volunteer with you in local clean-up or tree-planting projects.

- ♥ Take your family through the conservation inventory process in the activities above and plan to practice more earth-friendly daily habits at home, work and school.

- ♥ Make informed choices about what foods you eat, what products you buy, what entertainment you enjoy, how you use energy and how you dispose of used items based on the impact of those choices on the environment.

- ♥ Keep learning about the issues and expressing your informed views to your local paper, local government officials and national politicians.

Environmental Issues Word Search

Find and circle the bolded words on the grid below.
They may read up, down, across, diagonally or backwards.

```
E  S  L  E  F  X  E  A  M  S  D  D  Y  C  E
N  L  T  F  R  N  P  S  V  I  E  E  A  O  C
D  C  A  E  E  U  I  R  R  S  V  H  E  M  U
A  J  O  R  W  N  T  E  K  E  E  S  L  P  D
N  R  G  N  A  A  C  A  N  H  L  R  B  O  E
G  Y  E  G  S  Y  R  O  N  T  O  E  A  S  R
E  F  R  U  C  E  Z  D  J  N  P  T  N  T  R
R  O  N  L  S  O  R  Y  C  Y  M  A  I  C  Q
E  R  I  G  A  E  Z  V  M  S  E  W  A  R  R
D  N  E  G  Y  X  O  E  A  O  N  U  T  X  K
G  H  A  B  I  T  A  T  L  T  T  A  S  R  D
M  E  T  S  Y  S  O  C  E  O  I  F  U  R  S
S  O  L  A  R  D  G  W  S  H  V  O  S  M  Q
F  B  Q  Y  F  O  U  R  T  P  T  E  N  C  B
B  I  O  D  I  V  E  R  S  I  T  Y  L  M  F
```

biodiversity	compost	conservation
development	ecosystem	endangered
energy	habitat	nature
organism	oxygen	ozone
photosynthesis	recycling	reduce
reuse	solar	steward
sustainable	watershed	

Where Does the Garbage Go?

Complete the chart by listing common consumer products that you discard when you've finished with them. Use classroom, media center, public library or Internet resources to find out what happens to these products and ways they might be reused or recycled. An example has been provided to help get you started.

Product	Where does it go?	How can it be reused/recycled?
old car tires	Into a landfill or dumped into creeks or empty lots	Reconditioned for use as retreads or shredded or melted to make products like asphalt or soft playground surfaces

Aging and the Elderly

A fourth grade teacher recently told me about a class survey conducted in 1997, which indicated that only about 10% of her fourth graders had frequent contact with grandparents. While recent studies show a trend toward more extended family and three-generation households as the impact of newly immigrated families from diverse cultural backgrounds increases, many American children still grow up with little exposure to elderly people. At the same time we know that the average age of Americans is rising and that more retired or semi-retired seniors than ever before are exerting their influence in our communities. Both needs related to aging and the elderly and the dynamic and diverse resources of the senior population will affect the way today's children live even more profoundly than they have affected today's young and middle-aged adults. Our students have much to gain from being exposed to both these needs and resources.

Children isolated from the elderly often think of "old people" as strange, weak, unpleasant, cranky or useless and respond with discomfort or even fear, as you'll see in some of this chapter's books and media titles. What rich opportunities for learning compassion and empathy, benefiting from wisdom and experience and sharing friendship and service they miss! This arena offers particularly fertile ground for mutually satisfying and meaningful service-learning experiences, as students learn about the aging process from birth to death, offer service to the aging, make friends across generations and serve in tandem with senior citizens.

What are the issues of aging and the elderly in our communities, and how can we address them? These thoughts might help focus your studies.

♥ Defining senior citizens—Who are the elderly?

♥ What roles do senior citizens play in the community? Consider seniors who are working, semi-retired or retired but active, as well as those who are slowing down and more involved with health and end-of-life issues.

♥ Needs of the elderly in your community.

♥ Senior citizens as underused resources.

♥ How we benefit from close relationships with grandparents or elderly friends.

♥ Forms of discrimination that the elderly face—How can we better value senior citizens' knowledge and protect their pride, dignity and independence?

♥ What we can we learn from the elderly as they face end-of-life issues?

Resources on Aging and the Elderly

Use these resources to build knowledge and stimulate involvement in issues of aging.

Fiction

♥ ***Annie and the Old One*** by Miska Miles. Little, Brown and Company, 1985. K–5. Newbery Honor Book. Annie loves her Navajo grandmother. When Grandmother announces that she will die when the rug currently on the loom is completed, Annie tries to find ways to prevent its completion and hold onto the Old One. Grandmother sees through her schemes and explains the ways of sunrise, sunset, birth and death with wisdom and serenity.

♥ ***Doing Time Online*** by Jan Siebold. Albert Whitman, 2002. 2–5. As punishment for a scrape with the law involving a prank that endangered an elderly neighbor, Mitch has to "do time" in a chat room with a nursing home resident. What starts out as a resented chore turns into a friendship, as spunky "Wootie" and Mitch help each other face challenges in their lives.

♥ ***The Gawgon and the Boy*** by Lloyd Alexander. Penguin Putnam, 2002. 4–5. ALA Notable Children's Book. The Great Depression provides the setting for this witty, exciting story. David (the Boy) is tutored by his eccentric aunt (the Gawgon) while recovering from an illness. She shares an exciting world of books and ideas that stimulate him as school never has before. Snippets of heroes and legendary drama mix with routine events of daily life to produce wild, amusing, fantasy adventures in his vivid imagination. When the Gawgon dies, David must find ways to build her wisdom into his life.

♥ ***General Butterfingers*** by John Reynolds Gardiner. Penguin Putnam, 1993. 2–4. After the death of their commander-in-arms and benefactor General Britt, three elderly World War II veterans are about to lose their home to the General's greedy nephew. But, inspired and led by their young friend Walter, their famous rescue force "the Spitzers" takes on new life to foil the nephew's plan and save them from the dreaded Veteran's Hospital. This warm and wacky story showcases the irrepressible spirit of the vets and the power of intergenerational friendship.

♥ ***Great Aunt Martha*** by Rebecca C. Jones. Penguin Putnam, 1995. K–5. Great Aunt Martha's visit turns a child's world upside down as the family cleans, shops for sensible food and imposes silence so their guest can rest. But when Great Aunt Martha's had enough of the well-intended coddling, she rebels and the fun begins!

♥ ***The Magic Paintbrush*** by Laurence Yep. HarperCollins, 2003. 3–5. When Steve's parents die he has to move in with his stern, distant grandfather and his grumpy uncle in their rundown Chinatown tenement. He can't even enjoy his real love—painting—because there's no money for a new paintbrush. When Grandfather surprises him with a magic brush that makes anything real, Steve paints an adventure that helps the three discover their love for each other and the hopes and dreams they'd given up on.

♥ ***The Memory Box*** by Mary Bahr. Albert Whitman, 1995. 1–4. Zach spends summer vacations with his grandparents but this summer everything changes. Gramps has Alzheimer's disease and his behavior is increasingly erratic. Carrying on a family tradition of making a memory box helps the whole family reconcile with the reality of Gramps' illness and bleak future.

♥ ***Miz Berlin Walks*** by Jane Yolen. Penguin Putnam, 2000. K–5. Old Miz Berlin walks the neighborhood each evening, talking to herself. A little girl's curiosity gets the best of her and, despite her fear of the strange old woman, she takes up with her. The stories Miz Berlin weaves from her childhood and imagination form the fabric of a friendship. A spirited, sensitive look at elders as keepers of the legacy of oral tradition.

♥ ***Mr. Putter and Tabby Pick the Pears*** by Cynthia Rylant. Harcourt, 1995. 1–3. ALA Notable Children's Book. It's pear picking time and Mr. Putter can't wait for his pear jelly. But this year "cranky legs, cranky knees, cranky feet" make picking a challenge. Calling on ingenuity, childhood skills and, ultimately, some surprise assistance from his friend Mrs. Teaberry, Mr. Putter overcomes the obstacles in this delightful easy reader.

♥ **Mrs. Katz and Tush** by Patricia Polacco. Bantam Doubleday Dell, 1994. K–4. When Larnel finds a kitten in the basement of his apartment building, he decides to take it to his lonely elderly neighbor, Mrs. Katz. She agrees to keep him if Larnel will help and a lasting friendship is born. Larnel learns much from Mrs. Katz as they share their lives, customs and cultures, and he fills an empty place in her heart.

♥ **New Feet for Old** by Barrett Waller. Simon & Schuster, 1992. K–5. In this whimsical story of service and sacrifice an old peddler provides townspeople with young animal feet from his magic closet in trade for their tired, ailing feet, charging a kiss, joke or song. When he grows too old to continue his work he agrees to one last trade—his own sturdy feet to a crippled boy. The lovely surprise ending leaves readers free to enjoy both the magic and the pathos.

♥ **Old Bag of Bones: A Coyote Tale** by Janet Stevens. Holiday House, 1997. K–5. Old Coyote is "nothing but a bag of bones" but he's not ready to surrender to Buzzard yet. He convinces Young Buffalo to share his youth and strength, and is transformed into a young "buffote!" When he foolishly tries to overreach his new abilities by passing on youth to other old animals, he finds that they are not so eager to give up the wisdom, respect and experience they've earned. A witty, clever discussion-starter about the advantages of age.

♥ **Old People, Frogs, and Albert** by Nancy Hope Wilson. Farrar, Straus and Giroux, 1997. 2–4. Reluctant reader Albert is very sad when his elderly school reading buddy, Mr. Spear, has a stroke and winds up in a nursing home. His determination to honor the friendship and share his thanks and growing reading skills help Albert overcome his fear of the nursing home and its residents. A satisfying, quick read.

♥ **Pinky and Rex and the Mean Old Witch** by James Howe. Aladdin Paperbacks, 1999. 1–3. Pinky, his friend Rex and his sister Amanda plot to get back at the "mean old witch" next door after she chases them out of her yard. But Pinky's compassionate father starts Pinky thinking and he comes up with an alternate plan. A sweet, encouraging story.

♥ **The Special Gifts** by Peter Grosz. North-South Books, 1998. K–5. In this feast for the eyes picture book, three old men discover that building a comfortable, contented life is not enough. Old or not, they need to share their special talents and be of use in the world.

♥ **Stealing Home** by Mary Stolz. HarperCollins, 1994. 3–5. Ten-year-old Thomas and his grandfather have a cozy life in their little house with their pets and their shared love of fishing and baseball. Then Aunt Linzy comes to "visit," though it feels more like moving in and taking over. Thomas experiences trials and gains insights from living with his quirky aunt and wise grandfather. Baseball action and totally engaging characters widen the appeal of this charming story.

♥ **Verdi** by Janell Cannon. Harcourt Brace, 1996. K–5. With the rashness and irrepressibility of youth, Verdi, a tropical python, scorns the dullness of the green adult pythons' lives and vows to stay yellow and wildly adventurous forever. While time works its inevitable transformation on both color and temperament Verdi adjusts his sights to being himself and enjoying life. In equal parts, this visually stunning and delightful picture book educates us about snakes and attitudes toward aging.

♥ **The War with Grandpa** by Robert Kimmel Smith. Bantam Doubleday Dell, 1984. 3–5. Peter loves his grandpa, who has been lonely and sad since Grandma died. He's glad he's coming to live with the family—until he learns that Grandpa will take over his room! Peter decides to stand up for himself and declares a war (of practical jokes and minor harassment) to win back his room. To his surprise, Grandpa gets into the "war" in a way that helps him reconnect with the world, and helps Peter find a solution that's fair to everyone.

♥ **Wilfrid Gordon McDonald Partridge** by Mem Fox. Kane/Miller Book Publishers, 1995. K–2. Wilfrid lives next door to an old people's home and the residents are his friends. When his favorite resident starts losing her memory, Wilfrid sets out to learn what "memory" is and to help her restore it.

Nonfiction

♥ *Amos Fortune: Free Man* by Elizabeth Yates. Penguin USA, 1989. 4–5. Newbery Medal Book. This biography of a young African chieftain kidnapped into slavery in America doesn't reflect today's sensibilities but is a worthy addition just the same. Fortune worked with dignity, courage and determination to buy his freedom, which he finally did at age 60. He went on to buy several other African Americans out of slavery and become a role model for people of any age, gender or race.

♥ *Dr. Ruth Talks About Grandparents: Advice for Kids on Making the Most of a Special Relationship* by Dr. Ruth K. Westheimer with Pierre A. Lehu. Rowman & Littlefield Pub., 2001. 3–5. Dr. Ruth makes the case for developing close friendships with grandparents in a lively, engaging style. She shares fun, creative suggestions for strengthening ties with grandparents nearby and far away and also talks about finding "foster grandparents" and dealing with the death of a grandparent.

♥ *How Does It Feel to Be Old?* by Norma Farber. Creative Arts Book Company, 2001. K–5. Trina Schart Hyman's illustrations greatly enhance this frank, appealing book of poetic reflections of an elderly woman on an innocent question posed by her young granddaughter. The whole spectrum of positive and negative experiences and emotions touch us as we share in this legacy of life and family.

♥ *Images of Greatness: A Celebration of Life* by David Melton. Landmark Editions, 1987. 4–5. This unusual picture book features quotations from noted senior citizens past and present along with evocative pencil illustrations of many of those quoted. The quotations reflect all stages of life but emphasize the potential of and attitudes toward old age. Students might enjoy researching the fascinating elders represented, compiling wise quotes from senior citizens or sketching elderly people who are important in their lives.

Other Media

♥ *Lullabies of Love* by Roland-Story Rock-A-Bye Singers. Produced by Sue Twedt, 1998 (audiocassette). K–2. This tape was produced by the Helping Hands fourth graders and friends from Iowa mentioned in the Service-Learning in Action section on page 53. While not available through commercial sources, it deserves a place as an example of students working with seniors in service and for the songs and voices featured. Profits from purchases will support appropriate local charities identified by lead teacher Cindy Stull and her classes. To order the tape for $5.00 (including shipping and handling) contact:
Cindy Stull
515-733-4386
cstull@dns1.roland-story.k12.ia.us.

♥ *Tuck Everlasting* by Natalie Babbitt, read by Peter Thomas. Listening Library Inc., 1995 (audiocassettes). 4–5+. The Tuck family has long kept secret the magic of the spring water that stops aging and imparts immortality, anticipating terrible consequences if the public learns the truth. But when Winnie Foster happens upon them they must confide in her to safeguard the secret. What follows is a complex story of emotions and ethics told with dazzling lyricism and brilliant detail. Issues about "the wheel of life" are presented to and processed by the 10-year-old protagonist with credibility and integrity. This classic fantasy grabs you and won't let go!

Web sites

♥ *BrainPOP*
www.brainpop.com/health/growthand development/aging
Offers an interesting on-line movie on the cycle of life from birth through old age, for younger students.

♥ *National Grandparents Day WebQuest*
www.grandparents-day.net

♥ *Walk in My Shoes*
www.urbanext.uiuc.edu/wims/wimsproject.html
A 4–H Aging Awareness Project.

Here is an example of service-learning involving elementary students with the elderly in their community.

♥ **Helping Hands, Roland-Story Community School District, Iowa**
In 1993 fourth grade teacher Cindy Stull, of the Roland-Story Community School District in Iowa, began integrating service-learning into her curriculum throughout the year. By 1997–98 the program had evolved into its ongoing form, with Stull's fourth graders serving as "Helping Hands." Students work on team and community building early in the year. They develop a questionnaire, survey the community for perceived needs and plan projects to address those needs, grounding every activity solidly in the curriculum. A need identified in '97–'98 was a lack of interaction between children and senior citizens. Stull's class contacted the local RSVP (Retired & Senior Volunteers Program) and the Senior Citizen Center to find interested seniors. They worked with the school's first grade teacher Kris Hull. With all the individual players in place, they paired up first and fourth graders with senior "grandbuddies."

Interaction began as letter exchanges. As they explored Iowa history, students began to meet with their grandbuddies. The women worked with students to create embroidered baby quilts using historical themes, while some men taught students cribbage. The quilts were donated to local charities. One quilt went to the police department and is carried in a squad car to be used as needed with children encountered by officers on patrol.

The next initiative addressed skills and standards across the curriculum. It involved a close cooperation with the school's music department and was christened "The Lullaby Project." Students from nearby Wartburg College and music teacher Sue Twedt contributed original lullabies, while Kris Hull helped elementary students write lyrics to familiar melodies. Stull's students wrote original poems as part of a poetry unit and set them to music with help from district guidance counselor and recording artist Jane Todey. Todey and Twedt worked with students and grandbuddies, supplemented by the Senior Citizen Center Choir and other community members, at rehearsals and recording sessions. Students designed covers for the cassettes in class. The resulting tapes were copied and given to hospitals and new mothers, and were sold at conferences with proceeds going to a local shelter for abused women and children. In the spring the school held an intergenerational celebration as part of Helping Hands in which students and their grandbuddies sang, danced and spotlighted their shared activities and accomplishments during the year.

Stull reports that some buddy relationships formed in Helping Hands have lasted through the years and that she sees former students, confident they can have an impact, volunteering in the community throughout high school. In fact, it was through the insistence of Stull's former students that service-learning was introduced into the high school curriculum!

This ambitious, ongoing program demonstrates how deeply and effectively service-learning can pervade classroom instruction, as it evolves organically over time. To learn more about this complex, inspiring example of service-learning contact:
Cindy Stull
515-733-4386 at school
515-328-3235 at home
cstull@dns1.roland-story.k12.ia.us

Activities on Aging and the Elderly

Discussion Prompts

Use these prompts to explore issues of aging and the elderly.

♥ **Describing the Elderly.** Lead a brainstorming session on descriptive words to complete this sentence: "Elderly people are _____." This will shed light on perceptions and attitudes your class brings to the theme as you begin. After brainstorming, help students consider whether any of the descriptive words, positive or negative, apply to all elderly people or only to some. You might use examples of senior citizens students are likely to know, either from the school or local community or from the world of celebrities, or refer to the people depicted in *Images of Greatness: A Celebration of Life*. Then read *Old Bag of Bones: A Coyote Tale* together. Continue the discussion using these prompts:

- Animal characters in this story act like people, not animals, and are meant to represent people. What words from the brainstorming list describe Old Coyote (or Buffote)?

- What three things do Old Rabbit, Old Lizard and Old Kangaroo Rat like about being old? Are these things (wisdom, respect, experience) on our brainstorming list? Do they apply to some, or to all, elderly people?

- From the discussion, can the class come up with a brief paragraph that describes the elderly fairly? Why is this hard to do?

♥ **Book Discussions.** Assign small groups of students to read (or listen to) each of these titles: *The Magic Paintbrush, The War with Grandpa, Doing Time Online, The Gawgon and the Boy, General Butterfingers, Stealing Home* and *Tuck Everlasting*. Each group should choose one member to prepare a brief (2–3 minute) summary of the plot, character and issues of its book. Then pose these questions for students to respond to:

- What do you think the elderly characters in your books would say is the best thing about being older? (i.e., Grandfather's love for retirement in *Stealing Home*)

- What do you think those characters would say is the hardest thing about being older? (For example, Grandpa's sadness and loneliness after his wife's death in *The War with Grandpa*, having to give up your home as in *Doing Time Online* or the various health problems of "the Spitzers" in *General Butterfingers*.)

- What do you think Mr. Tuck, in *Tuck Everlasting*, would say to the elderly characters in the books about old age?

- Choose a character from your book and tell what you think that character would ask Steve to paint for him or her with the magic paintbrush.

- Suggest a fantasy adventure that the Boy, in *The Gawgon and the Boy*, might dream up based on *General Butterfingers*.

- What elderly character in your book (or what member of the Tuck family in *Tuck Everlasting*) would you like to know better and why?

Games

♥ **Acrostic Puzzles.** An acrostic puzzle is a word puzzle that can be read both up and down, and across. The letters of a word, written vertically, are used in other words or phrases written horizontally, to create a meaningful composition. Use the worksheet on page 59 to create acrostic compositions.

♥ **New Parts for Old.** Read *New Feet for Old* aloud. Point out that, while not all of the peddler's customers are old, age and long use begin to wear out our bodies so that most of us might, eventually, wish for the services of such a peddler to make our lives easier. Divide the class into teams, and assign each a body part (hands, eyes, legs, noses, etc.). Give them five minutes to think up problems people might have with that body part and what animal part from the magic closet might serve as a good substitute. For example, the team assigned eyes might list "eagle eyes for parents with many children to watch." After five minutes have each team share its ideas. The team with the most creative ideas might win a privilege like feeding the classroom pet for the week or being first in the recess line.

 **Creative Expressions**

Enjoy these creative ways to process concepts from books on the list.

♥ **Words of Wisdom Mobiles.** Have students collect 5–7 favorite wise sayings or words of advice from senior citizens (you might set a minimum age). Students might find some sayings in print sources or on the Internet, but at least half should come from talking to elderly people. Then collect materials and have students create mobiles featuring their Words of Wisdom as follows. See the illustration below.

Materials needed:
- sturdy paper plates (1 per student)
- assorted construction paper, card stock or heavy solid-colored wrapping paper
- crayons and felt-tip markers
- scissors
- colored yarn
- tape or stapler

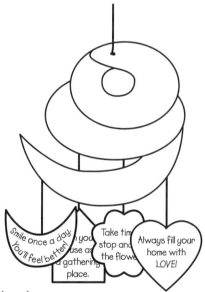

Directions:
- Color or otherwise decorate paper plates.

- Draw a spiral on the paper plates from an edge to the center and cut along the line, forming a coil.

- Attach a length of colored yarn to the center of the paper plate (now the top of the coil) for hanging up the mobile, using staples or tape.

- Cut appropriate shapes (books, hearts, etc.) for each "words of wisdom" saying from the assorted papers and write a saying on

each using markers. Remember to write the saying on both sides.

- Attach one or more sayings to each of three or more lengths of yarn with staples or tape so that they will hang down in interesting formations from the coil.

- Attach the lengths of yarn holding the sayings to the coil with staples or tape so that they form an attractive, balanced mobile.

♥ **When I was Your Age.** Assign students to interview a senior citizen, preferably a grandparent, other older relative or neighbor. Ask questions about what that person's life was like when he or she was the age of the student. Ask the senior to share a favorite story from his or her childhood and either take notes or record the story on tape. Students will bring their notes or tapes to class, write them in story form, illustrate them with original artwork and "bind" them in a folder. The stories can be given as thank-you gifts to the interviewed senior citizen.
Note: You might use this in conjunction with Oral Histories below.

♥ **When I Grow Old.** Have students imagine themselves at age 75 and write or tape-record letters to their grandchildren or great-grandchildren telling about their lives and offering advice. Invite willing students to share their letters with the class.

♥ **Intergenerational Portraits.** Using the illustrations in *Dr. Ruth Talks About Grandparents* or other books from this chapter bibliography, create a drawing or painting of a child and an elderly person doing something together that benefits both of them.

Research Opportunities

♥ **Oral Histories.** Perhaps in connection with a study of state or American history, assign students to interview an elderly person about his or her life as a child. Use the questionnaire on page 58 as an interview tool or create your own in consultation as a class. Students might take notes or record their interviews on tape. Work as a class to analyze responses to the questionnaire and create a chart identifying some of the main ways in which life was similar and different then and now.

♥ **Getting Around.** In this country, people travel almost everywhere by car. Whether it's going shopping, keeping doctor's appointments or visiting friends, most people use cars to get around. What happens to senior citizens when they can no longer drive a car because of vision or other problems? Research transportation options for the elderly or other non-drivers in your community. Look at bus routes and other public transportation as well as private transportation services. You might check the phone book under "Transportation," contact your local government for information or check with senior centers or other senior citizen service organizations. Are local services adequate to get senior citizens where they need to go? If not, talk about targeting this as a need to address through a class service-learning project.

♥ **Intergenerational Skills Swap.** Have students invite a grandparent, older relative or neighbor or adopted Senior Buddy to join them in a "skills swap." Student and senior should get together at least three times to teach each other something of mutual interest. Seniors might teach students a game, a dance, how to cook a favorite food or a craft like needlework or pottery. Students might teach seniors similar things from their own experience. Students should report back with a display or demonstration of skills shared.
Note: Many seniors could benefit from children's skill and confidence in using personal computers. Dr. Ruth Talks About Grandparents *includes a short chapter on "Grandparents and Computers."*

Miscellaneous Activities

♥ **Senior Buddies.** Contact a nearby nursing home or senior citizen center and collect names of seniors willing to be a "Senior Buddy" to a member of your class. Pair up students with senior buddies and have them exchange letters as pen pals. After a couple of letter exchanges, arrange a field trip for students to go to the nursing home or senior center and meet their buddies in person. They might start by performing a song as a class for all of the seniors and then have 15–20 minutes to visit one-on-one. Students might take a favorite or original story, poem or drawing to share with and give to their buddies as a starting place for their visits.

In Your Community

Use these starting points to discover needs and activity in your local community.

♥ Check out the phone book. Look in the yellow pages under headings like "Senior Citizens' Services" or "Retirement & Life Care Communities & Homes." Check government listings under "Community & Family Services—Senior Centers," "Department of Elder Affairs" or "Administration on Aging." Check to see if you have a chapter of RSVP (Retired & Senior Volunteer Program) in your community.

♥ Call your city hall or county supervisor's office and ask what agencies work with aging or senior citizen issues and what community organizations help.

♥ Search SERVEnet (www.servenet.org) for organizations that advocate for the elderly in your area.

♥ Watch the local newspapers and other publications for articles on how your community involves and serves its aging population.

♥ Talk to people "in the know" on this subject. They might be government employees or directors of service agencies like senior citizen centers or RSVP. You might invite such people to visit the class or assign students to practice communication, research and presentation skills by interviewing them and reporting back to the class. Find out what problems these people see that involve the elderly, and what the greatest needs in the community are.

Taking Action

Based on your research about issues involving aging and the elderly in your community, develop a plan for your service-learning project. These ideas might help you get started.

♥ Identify senior citizens needing help with house or yard work and organize a class workday to assist.

♥ Wage a campaign for improved transportation options for the elderly.

♥ Adopt "foster grandparents" or "senior buddies" and plan monthly service projects you can do together.

♥ Raise money to help support operating costs or provide needed supplies or materials for a local Senior Citizen Center.

♥ Research age discrimination in the workplace and write a letter to the editor of the local newspaper encouraging the community to value the experience of senior citizens.

♥ Identify the major health issues impacting the elderly and find ways to support research into cures or solutions

♥ Follow up oral history interviews with seniors by writing a play depicting either issues and problems of aging or childhood in an earlier era. Perform the play for your school and invite senior citizens to attend.

More Ideas

Share these ideas with motivated students who want to help as individuals.

♥ Visit or communicate with your own grandparents more often.

♥ Find out if there's a senior citizen in your neighborhood who could use some help with everyday chores and volunteer to help.

♥ Volunteer at a nursing home or other senior facility to read aloud, help write letters, sing, play games or just visit and listen.

♥ Ask your family to volunteer with you to deliver "Meals on Wheels" or to support local "Congregate Meals" sites.

♥ Spend time with your grandparents looking at old photo albums and sharing family stories, making a family tree, taping your family's history or watching movies together about an earlier time that they lived through.

♥ Find an elderly person who doesn't have family nearby and strike up a friendship! Invite him or her to your home for a meal, or to volunteer with you in the community.

♥ Keep learning about the issues and expressing your informed views to your local paper, local government officials and national politicians.

Oral History
Comparing Childhoods

Interview a senior citizen about his or her life as a child. Use this sheet to guide your interview and record responses.

I interviewed _____ **on this date** _____ .

The interview took place at _____ . **Here's what I learned.**

When and where were you born? Where did you grow up? Who was in your family?

What was your life like when you were my age? What were your jobs? Your friends? What did you do for fun?

Tell me about your school. How did you get to school? What did you learn?

Where did you shop? What did you eat? What did you buy?

Tell me one of your favorite stories from your childhood.

Aging & the Elderly Acrostic

An acrostic puzzle is a word puzzle that can be read both up and down, and across. The letters of a word, written vertically, are used in other words or phrases written horizontally, to create a meaningful composition. Take a look at the example provided, then try your hand at creating acrostic compositions from the words below.

Example

senio**R**
citiz**E**ns
de**S**erve
ap**P**reciation
h**E**lp
Courtesy and
respec**T**

G
R
A
N
D
M
A

G
R
A
N
D
P
A

A
G
I
N
G

W
I
S
D
O
M

Building Friendly Communities

All people live in communities of one kind or another. We come from families; live in neighborhoods; attend schools or participate in workplace communities; and reside in towns or counties, states, countries and the world. Many of us create our own families, participate in religious communities, are active in professional associations or interact with groups of likeminded friends. Even a recluse isolated from human society can't avoid being part of a natural community of plants and animals and a resident of planet Earth. How does living in communities help us? What gives us a positive sense of community? What are the obstacles to openness, cooperation and friendly attitudes in a community?

While we share so many similarities as humans living in this world, it seems that most of the challenges of living and working together in communities come from trying to understand and deal with differences among community members. We are different from one another in many ways—gender, age, race, religion, physical limitations, ethnicity. More subtly, our attitudes and habits resulting from family, cultural traditions or educational background can set us at odds with one another. Ignorance can lead to stereotyping, prejudice and discrimination. In this chapter we'll look at what communities mean to people, issues of local and global citizenship, the "isms" that get in the way and strategies for building and nurturing friendly communities.

What are the challenges to friendliness and cooperation in your community, and what can we do about them? These topics might help focus your exploration.

- ♥ Communities we belong to.

- ♥ How communities help us—What are the benefits of living in communities?

- ♥ Being good citizens, locally and globally.

- ♥ Similarities that define our communities and differences that cause tension in them.

- ♥ How does a friendly community look, feel and act?

- ♥ Experiences that bring communities together.

- ♥ Stereotypes, prejudice and discrimination—How can we resist them?

Resources on Building Friendly Communities

Use these titles to explore and stimulate interest in supporting friendly communities.

✋ Fiction

♥ ***And to Think That We Thought That We'd Never Be Friends*** by Mary Ann Hoberman. Bantam Doubleday Dell, 2003. K–2. From a sibling battle to a worldwide parade, this riotous celebration of a picture book looks at how offering to share and inviting others in can overcome obstacles and make friends of strangers. The unifying power of music is featured.

♥ ***Bein' with You This Way*** by W. Nikola-Lisa. Lee & Low Books, 1995. K–2. A young African American girl leads an urban-rap style celebration of diversity in a neighborhood park.

♥ ***The Car Washing Street*** by Denise Lewis Patrick. William Morrow & Co., 1993. K–3. It's Saturday and Matthew can't wait to get outside. This vibrant picture book celebrates a tradition of shared work and play in an ethnically diverse neighborhood.

♥ ***The Chalk Box Kid*** by Clyde Robert Bulla. Random House, 1987. 1–3. Gregory's family has fallen on hard times and moved to a run-down house in a neighborhood of concrete. Off to a rocky start at his new school, Gregory consoles himself by creating a chalk garden on the walls of a burned-out building. A sensitive story about the healing and unifying power of creating beauty in unexpected places.

♥ ***A Day for Vincent Chin and Me*** by Jacqueline Turner Banks. Houghton Mifflin, 2001. 3–5. Tommy is worried and uncomfortable when his mother agrees to speak at a rally supporting the rights of Asian Americans, calling attention to his Japanese background. At the same time Tommy and his "posse" of bright, ethnically diverse buddies are taking their own drastic social action to make their street safer for children. Likable, believable characters and satisfying plot resolution make this a winner.

♥ ***Glenna's Seeds*** by Nancy Edwards. Child Welfare League of America, 2000. K–3. This warm, richly illustrated picture book tells how Glenna's gift of flower seeds starts a chain reaction of anonymous gifts and acts of kindness in her neighborhood.

♥ ***Grandpa's Corner Store*** by DyAnne DiSalvo-Ryan. William Morrow & Co., 2000. K–5. When a big supermarket moves in near her grandpa's grocery store Lucy worries that her grandpa may be forced out of business. She rallies the neighbors, many of whom have benefited from Grandpa's kind heart and personal service, to give the store a facelift and a fighting chance.

♥ ***Jackie & Me*** by Dan Gutman. William Morrow & Co., 2000. 3–5. In this time travel adventure Joe Stoshak travels to 1947 to research a class assignment about Jackie Robinson. He is startled to find that he's also been transformed into a black boy, and shares in Robinson's experiences of racism during the baseball great's rookie season. Lots of baseball action keeps the reader riveted as memorable lessons about the evils of prejudice and the triumph of human dignity emerge.

♥ ***Nothing Ever Happens on 90th Street*** by Roni Schotter. Scholastic, 1999. 1–5. Eva is an aspiring writer but bemoans the fact that nothing happens in her neighborhood to write about. That changes one day when everyone gives Eva advice, and circumstances conspire to make <u>everything</u> happen on 90th Street! A striking, whimsical look at how things improve when people get involved and share ideas.

♥ ***Ola Shakes It Up*** by Joanne Hyppolite. Random House, 2001. 3–5. It's 9-year-old Ola's role in life to shake things up. So when her family becomes the first black family in an upscale-but-uptight housing development full of rules, she's just the person to challenge the status quo. Spunky Ola finds a team of free-spirited conspirators and does just that. A fun read with just enough substance.

♥ ***Raising Yoder's Barn*** by Jane Yolen. Little, Brown and Company, 2002. K–5. Rich, earth tone paintings by Bernie Fuchs reinforce the simple message as the Yoders' Amish neighbors join to help when their barn burns down. A fine example of a cooperative, caring community at work.

♥ **See You Around, Sam!** by Lois Lowry. Bantam Doubleday Dell, 1998. 2–4. When 4-year-old Sam's mother won't let him wear his vampire fangs in the house, what can he do but run away to Alaska? In this adventure of Anastasia Krupnik's family the whole neighborhood conspires to keep Sam safe and change his mind without appearing to resist his plans.

♥

♥ **Smoky Night** by Eve Bunting. Harcourt Brace, 1999. K–5. Caldecott Medal Book. Bunting shares a night of rioting, looting and arson in an inner city neighborhood. Neighbors of different backgrounds have stayed aloof from each other, preferring to associate with "their own." But the tragic events bring people together and open the door to new trust and friendship. Glorious, vibrant paintings and collages by David Diaz capture all the drama, violence and hope of the story.

♥

♥ **Some Good News** by Cynthia Rylant. Simon & Schuster, 2001. 2–4. This light, happy reader in The Cobblestone Cousins series features Lily, Tess and Rosie as they celebrate the neighborhood where they live with their Aunt Lucy by creating a community newsletter.

♥ **What Zeesie Saw on Delancey Street** by Elsa Okon Rael. Aladdin Paperbacks, 2000. 1–5. ALA Notable Children's Book. At seven, Zeesie is old enough to attend her first "package party"—a fundraiser enjoyed by Jewish immigrants to help bring others from their native villages to America. There Zeesie spies on the secret tradition of the money room, where she learns about generosity and dignity. A beautiful and touching story about taking care of each other in communities.

♥

Nonfiction

♥ **Cliques, Phonies & Other Baloney** by Trevor Romain. Free Spirit Publishing, 1998. 3–5. Witty, informal text and lighthearted cartoon illustrations add appeal to this little book that tells the truth about cliques and friendship. It focuses on a school setting, but has much to say about what makes for friendly communities anywhere.

♥

♥ **Dealing with Racism** by Jen Green. Millbrook Press, 1998. K–3. This How I Feel About series title uses simple language, eye-catching design, cartoon illustrations and

color photos to explain racism and its impact on five real children to young students. It is a bit simplistic and includes religious and cultural intolerance along with prejudice based on skin color under the term racism, but is useful for beginning to present facts and advice about this all-too-pervasive attitude in our communities.

♥ **Exploring Our World: Neighborhoods and Communities** by Kathleen M. Hollenback. Scholastic Professional Books, 2000. 1–3. This teacher resource book offers literature tie-ins, a skit, a game and other activities including reproducibles for introducing basic concepts of community. Emphasis is on what community means, different kinds of communities and appreciating community services and helpers.

♥ **Melting Pot or Not? Debating Cultural Identity** by Paula A. Franklin. Enslow Publishers, 1995. 4–5. This balanced, accessible title in Enslow's Multicultural Issues series explores America as a nation of immigrants, and the various models and approaches we have brought to dealing with cultural and ethnic diversity. It spotlights the experiences of African Americans, Hispanic Americans and Native Americans and poses thoughtful questions that invite open discussion.

♥ **More New Games and Playful Ideas** edited by Andrew Fluegelman. Doubleday & Company, 1981. K–5. While no longer in print, this book and its earlier companion *The New Games Book* are still widely available in libraries. And though the illustrations and some of the text are dated for today's readers, the basic concept of games based on cooperation and fun as opposed to competition and winning is a useful one. You might use specific games in the classroom or on the playground and talk about the attitudes they promote in the context of community building.

♥ **Quilted Landscape: Conversations with Young Immigrants** by Yale Strom. Simon & Schuster, 1996. 3–5. Strom shares comments and experiences of 26 young recent immigrants from around the world. Black-and-white photos and effective design, including rich sidebar details about the subjects' countries of origin, invite readers to meet these interesting, outspoken youth. Common threads in their stories include appreciation for opportunity and diversity in the U.S. and frank criticism of violence and racism. Their strong voices could stimulate honest discussion of what's best and worst about our communities.

♥ ***Tales Alive! Ten Multicultural Folktales with Activities*** by Susan Milord. Williamson Publishing, 1994. 1–5. This richly illustrated collection offers lots of background and cultural context for tales both new and familiar from around the world. Milord suggests several activities connected to each story, with clear directions. In addition to supporting appreciation for diverse cultures, two of the stories, "A Drum" and "Why Hare is Always on the Run," convey messages about working effectively in communities.

♥ ***Under Our Skin: Kids Talk About Race*** by Debbie Holsclaw Birdseye and Tom Birdseye. Holiday House, 1997. 1–5. Like *Quilted Landscape,* this picture book gives voice to young people of varied ethnicity talking about their experiences with diversity in their communities. Color photos and longer segments feature fewer young people, with a narrower focus on race and racism. Again, frankness and a variety of experiences and mindsets make this title interesting and form a credible snapshot of American cultural attitudes.

Other Media

♥ ***Mrs. Frisby and the Rats of Nimh*** by Robert C. O'Brien, narrated by Barbara Caruso. Recorded Books, 1993 (audiocassettes). 4–5. Newbery Medal Book. Caruso effectively reads the unabridged classic in which Mrs. Frisby, knowing her mouse family is in danger, seeks help from the mysteriously advanced rats of Nimh and does the rats a priceless service in return.

♥ ***Yo! Yes?*** by Chris Raschka, narrated by Ryann Williams and Tucker Bliss, music composed by Jerry Dale McFadden. Orchard Books, 1993; Weston Woods, 2000 (book and audiocassette). K–2. Caldecott Honor Book. The upbeat, city-rhythms soundtrack perfectly complements this sparse, stunning picture book about the beginnings of a friendship. You'll snap your fingers along for the joy of it!

Web sites

♥ ***The Colors of Courage***
home.att.net/~RWfreebird/

♥ ***Kids Next Door***
www.hud.gov/kids/

♥ ***The Mosaic of Immigrants to America: Foundation of a Multicultural Society***
library.thinkquest.org/19258/

♥ ***Peace Corps Kids World***
www.peacecorps.gov/kids/
The Peace Corps Web site also offers lesson plans exploring prejudice, stereotypes and peace-related issues.

Here are some examples of service-learning projects in which elementary school students supported and nurtured strong, friendly communities.

♥ **Fourth of July Musical Pageant, Southeast Warren Community School District, Iowa**

In the summer of 1999 elementary and middle school students from the Southeast Warren Community School District worked to present a Fourth of July musical pageant celebrating the history of its three district communities, Lacona, Liberty Center and Milo, Iowa. Under the direction of music teacher Lynnea Young, students interviewed local senior citizens; wrote skits; developed costumes, sets and props; and performed the skits for the district population. The project grew out of a period of tension among the district's member communities over school issues and provided an opportunity for students to help bring the communities together while consolidating skills in a variety of curricular areas. To learn more about this creative initiative contact:

> Lynnea Young
> 641-466-3694
> lyoung@se-warren.k12.ia.us

♥ **Knowledge Builds Respect and Peace Mural, Plymouth, Minnesota**

Art teacher Diana Klisch and professional artist Marilyn Lindstrom teamed up in April 2002 to help nearly 100 fifth graders at Oakwood Elementary School in Plymouth, Minnesota, learn while creating a public mural as a gift from their class to the school. Addressing curriculum standards in cultural studies, history, art and language arts, Klisch

arranged for Lindstrom, who specializes in murals with multicultural themes, to work as artist-in-residence with her students. The school's PTA sponsored the residency. Lindstrom guided students to explore their own cultural backgrounds and the cultures represented in the school. Students worked from prepared visual resource packets of artwork from African, European, Asian, Native American and MesoAmerican heritages, composing individual designs incorporating all five cultural areas. The project evolved through a process of individual work, small group compositions, evaluation of the collective body of drawings and, finally, the design and creation of a mural on a wall outside the school media center. One of five students who presented speeches at a dedication ceremony commented, "By learning about each other's culture, we start to understand each other and respect and appreciate our differences." Students were excited and enthusiastic about the project, which was followed by both in-school and local media. The result—a friendlier and more beautiful school community! For more information contact:

> Diana Klisch or
> Oakwood Principal Paula Martin
> Oakwood Elementary
> 17340 County Road 6
> Plymouth, MN 55447
> 763-745-5700
> diana_klisch@wayzata.k12.mn.us.
>
> Marilyn Lindstrom
> 612-825-1859
> murals@bitstream.net

Activities on Building Friendly Communities

Discussion Prompts

Use these prompts to stimulate discussion of community building issues.

♥ **Similarities and Differences.** Much tension and conflict in communities—from families to nations—comes when we don't focus on our similarities or appreciate our differences. Choose one or more books from the chapter (*The Chalk Box Kid, Ola Shakes It Up, A Day for Vincent Chin and Me, Mrs. Frisby and the Rats of Nimh, And to Think That We Thought That We'd Never Be Friends* or *Smoky Night* could be used here) for the class to read. Then lead a discussion:

• What are the main problems in the story?

• How are the characters in the story alike? What things do they share? What similarities among them do they ignore?

• How are the characters different? What differences between characters add to the problems? Are any characters afraid of each other because they are different?

• How are the problems resolved? Do the solutions have to do with getting to know each other better, seeing similarities and appreciating differences?

• What community is better at the end of the book, and how is it better?

♥ **Competition vs. Cooperation.** Another source of conflict in communities is a pervasive attitude of competition rather than cooperation. Explore these ideas with the class:

• Look up "competition" and "cooperation" in a dictionary and write the definitions on the board. Emphasize that competition implies winners and losers and cooperation emphasizes working together for mutual benefit.

• What are some examples of activities in which we usually compete? Cooperate? Look for examples from the books as well as from real life.

• What's good about competition? What's bad about it? How does it feel to be the winner? The loser? Is there anyone who always wins in competitive activities? Does anyone always lose?

• What's good about cooperation? What's bad about it? How does it feel when everyone works together to benefit the group?

• Do you think competition or cooperation does more to make your family, classroom or local community feel friendly?

• Can you have as much fun being cooperative as you can being competitive?

• How can we stress cooperation more in the classroom?

• Cap off the discussion by playing one or more of the games from *More New Games and Playful Ideas* and noting how it demonstrates a cooperative approach.

♥ **Stereotypes.** When we don't know people in our communities, it's easy to lump them together with other people who are similar in some way and to make judgments about them without knowing them. This is called "stereotyping." For example, you might have heard people say that "Boys are stronger than girls," that "People with blonde hair aren't very smart" or even that "Poor people are lazy." Discuss these questions about stereotyping.

• What other stereotypes about people have you heard? (Remind the class to use appropriate language and consider the feelings of others in the room as they share.)

• Are stereotypes true? Are they false? Do they apply to some or all people in a group?

• Have you ever been stereotyped by others rather than seen as your individual self? How does that feel?

• Have you ever judged others because of a group you think they belong to, without knowing them? Why or why not?

• Why are stereotypes harmful? How do they hurt the person who is stereotyped? How do they hurt the person doing the stereotyping?

• Look up the words "prejudice" and "discrimination." What do these things have to do with stereotyping? There's a good section on these concepts in Chapter 2 of *Melting Pot or Not?* They are also explored in *Dealing with Racism, Under Our Skin* and *Quilted Landscapes.*

♥ **Communities Responding to Crisis.**
Raising Yoder's Barn, Smoky Night and *Mrs. Frisby and the Rats of Nimh* talk about communities coming together after something bad happens. Share one of these stories and consider these prompts:

- What bad thing happened that brought the community together in these stories?

- What did people do in response to the crisis in their community? How did they work together and help each other?

- Can you think of other times when something bad that happened helped make a community stronger and friendlier?

- Why is it that shared crises seem to bring people together?

Games

♥ **Mystery Word.** Enjoy the mystery word puzzle on the handout on page 70, using words and ideas that relate to building friendly communities. The mystery word is "cooperate."

♥ **In Groups, Out Groups.** This game explores inclusive vs. exclusive attitudes toward social interaction. You might use *Cliques, Phonies & Other Baloney* as you process the experience. Divide the class into groups of 8–10 students. You'll need an appropriate joke book or other simple, fun activity for each group and 15–25 index cards listing inclusion/exclusion criteria prepared in advance. Each card should specify some obvious, superficial criterion for "who's in" and "who's out." For example, one card might read "Who's in: Anyone with Velcro-fastened shoes. Who's out: Everyone else!" Or "Who's out: Anyone with red hair. Who's in: Anyone who doesn't have red hair."

For each round of play, pick a card and give it to a player who, by the card's definition, is "in." (For example, give the second example above to a black-haired student.) That player is the "in-group leader" and uses the criterion on the card to choose two others in the group who are also "in." Those two players read from the joke book or do something else simple and fun. Remaining students get one guess each as to what defines "in" that round. If no one guesses, the leader chooses another student to be "in." That student joins the fun; the others guess again. Continue until some-

one identifies the criterion or until everyone is stumped. If a group runs out of students who meet the "in" criterion before the answer is guessed, allow a final round of guesses. If the play ends and the group has not guessed, the leader reads the card aloud. Then the teacher chooses another card, gives it to a different "in" player to be the leader of that group, and the process repeats.

Continue the game until most students in each group have experienced being both "in" and "out," and several have been "leader." Then gather the class and talk about the experience.

- How did it feel to be in the "in group"? The "out group"? How did it feel to be the leader of the "in group"?

- Are these ways of choosing whom to include fair or unfair? Why?

- Would you choose your friends based on criteria like those on the cards? Why or why not?

- How do you decide whom to include or exclude?

- Are your criteria fairer than those on the cards? Why or why not?

- Can others tell what criteria define who's "in" or "out" of the social circles in your class or school?

- Who decides who's "in" or "out" of those circles?

Creative Expressions

Enjoy these creative ways to process concepts from books on the list.

♥ **"Bein' With You."** *Bein' with You This Way, Grandpa's Corner Store* and *The Car Washing Street* celebrate something special about a neighborhood. Review these books with the class. Then invite students to complete one of these assignments:

- Think of something special that your family, class, neighborhood or town does together, like Saturday morning car washing. Write or tape-record a short story about the event or activity and illustrate it. Share your story with the class.

- Think of a place you like to go to be with other people, like the park in *Bein' with You This Way* or *Grandpa's Corner Store*. Write or tape-record a poem or song about that place and the people you enjoy there. Share it with the class.

♥ **Defining Friendly Communities.** Begin this unit by putting up a large piece of paper on a classroom or hallway wall. Write in large letters at the top, "What Makes a Friendly Community?" During the unit invite students to write, draw or paste onto the paper words and images that relate to building friendly communities. They might include words that define communities, like "neighborhood," "world," "church," etc. They might draw or cut and paste pictures of people working together. They might editorialize using phrases like "No Racism!" or "Respect Everyone." By the end of the unit you should have a collage that summarizes students' understanding.

♥ **Musical Expression.** Have students work in pairs or small groups to write new lyrics to a familiar melody, sharing a message about overcoming prejudice in our communities.

♥ **Dramatic Challenge.** Introduce the book *Tales Alive! Ten Multicultural Folktales with Activities.* Invite individual students to prepare dramatic readings of the stories or groups of students to present stories as skits with costumes and props. You might also have the class do some of the activities or craft projects connected with the stories.

Research Opportunities

♥ **Celebrating Diversity.** Find out what national, cultural and ethnic groups are represented in your school. You might develop a simple survey to have each class complete. If you live in a diverse community it may be easy to spot ethnic groups who identify with their backgrounds. In a less diverse community you may have to survey students' families to identify more distant immigrant roots and cultural backgrounds. When you have an idea of the cultures in your community, plan activities to learn about and celebrate those cultures.

♥ **Local History Exploration.** Study the history of your local community. Use the worksheet on page 71 to guide your research. You might have each student complete the entire worksheet or divide the class into groups to explore subsections of the worksheet in more depth.

After gathering and sharing information discuss as a class the final question.

♥ **Community Spirit in Sports.** *Jackie & Me* shares history about the integration of sports in America which sheds light on sports teams as a form of community, for better or worse. Invite students to research the lives and careers of favorite sports figures, stressing their performance in the areas of teamwork and sportsmanship. Have students present reports including pictures of their athletes, ideas about how they demonstrate community spirit and, if possible, quotes from them about the importance of working cooperatively with others.

Miscellaneous Activities

♥ **Anonymous Gifts.** Both *What Zeesie Saw on Delancey Street* and *Glenna's Seeds* talk about what happens in a community when people receive anonymous gifts. Review these stories. Then write the names of each student in the class on slips of paper and place them in a container. Have each student draw a name. Within a week, students are to do one anonymous act of kindness for the classmate whose name they drew. Encourage them not to get caught! After the week is over talk about what happened and how anonymous acts of kindness affected individuals and the feeling of community in the class.

♥ **Citizen of the Month.** Create a bulletin honoring a school Citizen of the Month. Set up a process for nominating and selecting a member of the school community to be honored for demonstrating outstanding school spirit. Invite the whole school to participate.

♥ **International Pen Pals.** Give students a chance to get involved as citizens of the world by making friends with an international pen pal. These organizations can make the connection:

Peace Pals
26 Benton Rd.
Wassaic, NY 12592
845-877-6093
www.worldpeace.org/peacepals.html

World Pen Pals
P.O. Box 337
Saugerties, NY 12477
845-246-7828
www.world-pen-pals.com

Building Friendly Communities Right Here

In Your Community

Use these starting points to discover needs and activity in your local community.

♥ Check out the phone book. See if there's a "Community Pages" section that features various services and cultural attractions in your community. Look through your local government listings to see what services are offered that represent people working together to make life better for everyone.

♥ Call your city hall or county supervisor's office and ask what agencies work with community building issues and what community organizations help. See if your city council, school district, public library or museum has a student or youth board that involves children in providing community services.

♥ Check out SERVEnet (www.servenet.org) to see what organizations are addressing these issues in your area.

♥ Watch local newspapers and other publications for articles on how people work to make communities more open, friendly and cooperative.

♥ Talk to people "in the know" on this subject. They might be government employees or members of nonprofit organizations like a Citizens for Community Improvement group or an International Club. You might invite these resource people to visit the class or assign students to practice communication, research and presentation skills by interviewing them and reporting back. Find out what they see as the greatest challenges to creating and nurturing friendliness, cooperation and inclusiveness in your community.

Taking Action

Based on your research about community building issues in your area, plan a service-learning project. These ideas might get you started.

♥ Start a campaign to pass a "Community Beautification Day" proclamation and promote beautification projects in your town.

♥ Work to save a valued local business threatened by a mega-business, as Lucy did in *Grandpa's Corner Store*.

♥ Work with professional artists in creating a work of public art to add beauty to an unsightly area of town. Try to involve residents or business people from the area.

♥ If your town doesn't already have a community festival that celebrates its unique history and spirit, build on your work in Celebrating Diversity on page 67 to plan and sponsor such a festival with a goal of building appreciation, cooperation and community spirit.

♥ Build on your findings about cultural and ethnic diversity in your school to plan and sponsor a community-wide celebration of diversity. This could take the form of an international food and crafts fair or a performance of ethnic music, dance and storytelling.

♥ Create a school newspaper to encourage cooperation, service, friendly attitudes and school spirit. You might get some ideas of what to include from *Some Good News*.

♥ Create and prepare a series of skits about prejudice and discrimination for a school assembly, to raise awareness and start conversation about the importance of tolerance and cooperation. Remember to address a wide range of differences (disabilities, ages, ethnicity, etc.) in your skits. The scenarios presented in *Dealing with Racism* might provide a starting point.

♥ Participate as a class in a community clean-up day.

♥ Start a diversity club in your school to celebrate differences and address issues of stereotypes, prejudice and discrimination in students' lives.

More Ideas

Share these ideas with motivated students who want to help as individuals.

♥ Ask your parents to help you host a block party to get to know and strengthen ties with your neighbors.

- ♥ Keep your eyes open for problems that divide people in your community and think of ways you can help address them.

- ♥ Volunteer for an organization that supports community building or provides an important community service, like a library or local history museum.

- ♥ Encourage your parents to vote on local and national issues.

- ♥ Keep learning about the issues and expressing your informed views to your local paper, local government officials and national politicians.

Mystery Word Game

Solve the puzzle by first filling in the missing words using the word bank. Then unscramble the letters in parentheses to find the mystery word.

Word Bank

citizens	family	together
prejudice	involved	respect
differences	similar	benefit

1. When you get to know people you find that they are more __ __ __ __ __ __ (___) than they are different from each other.

2. A __ (___) __ __ __ __ is a community made up of parents, children and other relatives.

3. When you judge someone without knowing him or her as an individual you are showing (___) __ __ __ __ __ __ __ __.

4. We are all __ __ __ __ __ (___) __ __ of the communities we belong to.

5. People in friendly communities combine their efforts for the __ __ __ __ __ __ (___) of everyone.

6. If we don't learn to appreciate __ __ __ __ __ __ __ __ (___) __ __ between people we will have conflict in our communities.

7. Friendly communities happen when people get __ __ __ (___) __ __ __ __ and work together.

8. Good communities make rules that __ __ __ __ (___) __ __ every person.

9. Part of being a community is working __ (___) __ __ __ __ __ __ for the good of all.

Unscramble the letters in parentheses to find the mystery word. Write it below.

__ __ __ __ __ __ __ __ __

Community History Worksheet

Organize your research on your community's history and character using this sheet.

Visit your local public library or local history organization.

A. Ask for help finding books, articles or other records of your town's history.

B. Using library resources, look for information to fill in the blanks below.

1. When was the town founded? _____

2. Who first founded it? _____

3. Why? (As a trading center for area farmers, a railroad stop, a port on a waterway, a coal-mining town, etc.) _____
_____

4. Were there earlier inhabitants of the area? Who? _____
_____

5. What kinds of businesses have supported the local economy through the years?
_____
_____

6. What families have lived in the area for many years or generations?
_____

7. Are there any famous people who came from the town? Who?
_____

8. What events of historic interest happened in or near the town?
_____
_____

9. What else is the town known for? (Any famous buildings, legends, natural features or landmarks, etc.) _____
_____

Contact local government.

A. Ask an appropriate town employee for help finding this information.

1. When was the town legally incorporated? _____

2. What is the structure of local government? (Mayor/Council, etc.)
_____

3. Has the form of government changed during the town's history? Why?
_____
_____

4. Does the town offer any unusual services? What? _____

5. When are there open town meetings? Do many people attend them?
   _____

6. Are there former mayors or other people active in local government who could talk about what's special about the town? Who?_____

7. What's the most important thing that's ever happened in the town? _____
   _____

Interview a community member.

A. From the sources above, identify one or more people who have lived in the community and been active in community affairs for many years.

B. Arrange to interview that person or those people, using these questions or others you think will be interesting.

1. How long have you lived in the community? _____

2. Did your relatives live here before you? For how long? _____
   _____

3. What community activities have you been involved in?_____
   _____

4. What is your favorite memory of this community? _____
   _____
   _____

5. What do you think is the most important thing that ever happened here?
   _____
   _____

6. What do you think is unusual or special about this community?
   _____
   _____

7. Do you plan to stay here? Why or why not? _____
   _____

After completing the worksheet, write a sentence or two below that answers this question: What's special about my community?

_____
_____
_____
_____
_____

© 2003 by Diane Findlay (UpstartBooks)

Literacy and Education

It's fact as well as cliché that life is all about learning, and in a society like ours learning is largely about reading. When it comes to promoting education and literacy we tend to think of children as being on the receiving side of the equation. How can elementary students support and serve the ideals of literacy and life-long learning? In this chapter we look at students coming to appreciate the educational opportunities they have and to respect and support the people who provide them. We see students helping each other across age, grade and ability lines to learn important skills and attitudes. We explore differences in the ways people learn and see elementary students helping adults and senior citizens to be lifelong learners. We get a glimpse of some of the things educators can learn from their students. A service-learning approach to issues of literacy and education provides wonderful opportunities for students to extend themselves in service right in their own school communities.

The books in this chapter also explore some pitfalls inherent in a formal education setting like excessive competition, the temptation to cheat or the perception of unfair treatment by teachers who single out students for too much negative or positive attention.

What are the most pressing problems related to literacy and education in your community, and how can you address them? These ideas might help focus your exploration of literacy and education.

♥ How to instill appreciation and respect for teachers and the learning process.

♥ Sharing information, skills and attitudes in formal and informal settings.

♥ Different learning styles.

♥ Learning disabilities and attitudes toward LD students.

♥ English as a Second Language.

♥ The scope and impact of the problem of illiteracy in the U.S. and around the world.

♥ Efforts to reduce illiteracy and innumeracy in the U.S. and around the world.

♥ The power of learning by teaching including tutoring, peer tutoring and mentoring.

♥ The importance of lifelong learning.

Resources on Literacy and Education

Use these titles to explore and stimulate interest in literacy and education.

Fiction

♥ ***Aunt Chip and the Great Triple Creek Dam Affair*** by Patricia Polacco. Putnam, 1996. K–5. The folks in Triple Creek love TV so much that they have given up using books for anything but doorstops and building material. Aunt Chip hasn't left her bed for 50 years in protest. When Aunt Chip discovers people have forgotten how to read she rallies to right the heinous wrong. This whimsical picture book celebrates the benefits and pleasures of reading and learning.

♥ ***Barry*** by Bruce Brooks. HarperCollins, 1999. 4–5. While Barry's passion for hockey waxes his interest in academics wanes. To avoid dire consequences he must convince his teacher mother that he respects the learning process. He devises a plan to systematically share his hockey skills with an inexperienced but gifted teammate and is surprised to discover the rewards of teaching on the ice and learning in the classroom. Lots of hockey action and a sophisticated style make this Wolfbay Wings series title appealing to sports fans who are mature readers.

♥ ***Fourth Grade Weirdo*** by Martha Freeman. Random House, 2001. 3–5. This celebration of weirdness embraces two delightful, believable characters—a nerdy kid and a creative, dedicated teacher—as each faces difficult challenges. Mr. Ditzwinkle must beat a bum rap as a thief and Dexter must learn to be true to himself. A zany and perceptive look at teaching and learning on several levels.

♥ ***In Trouble with Teacher*** by Patricia Brennan Demuth. Penguin Putnam, 1995. 1–3. Montgomery hasn't studied his spelling words, and fears that tough Mrs. Wix will be mad at him. While it's hard to tell if this story is about laziness or a learning disability, Mrs. Wix's unexpected kindness and understanding are admirable and motivating. An entertaining read.

♥ ***Jake Drake Teacher's Pet*** by Andrew Clements. Aladdin Paperbacks, 2001. 2–4. Fourth grader Jake recounts four terrible days in third grade when he became, through no fault of his own, teacher's pet. This funny, easy read about an ordinary kid facing the dragons of elementary school social life carries interesting messages about the dangers of teachers singling out students for special attention, positive or negative.

♥ ***Jeremiah Learns to Read*** by Jo Ellen Bogart. Scholastic, 1999. K–5. Old Jeremiah can do many things well, but he never learned to read. In this heartwarming picture book tribute to lifelong learning the children and teacher in a one-room school welcome Jeremiah and share an adventure of teaching and learning.

♥ ***Just Juice*** by Karen Hesse. Scholastic, 1999. 4–5. Juice's loving but hard-luck family struggles to make ends meet. Juice, who has trouble in school and prefers to help her father at home, feels the weight of their problems. When a series of crises strikes, Juice's learning difficulties and her father's illiteracy are exposed. A daunting look at the grinding impact of poverty and illiteracy tempered by characters you can't help caring about. The birth of Juice's sister, in which Juice must assist, is described in fairly explicit detail.

♥ ***Mary Marony and the Chocolate Surprise*** by Suzy Kline. Penguin Putnam, 1995. 1–3. When nasty Marvin draws the winning chocolate bar in a contest to eat with Mary's favorite teacher, Mary gives in to temptation and switches her candy for his. But Mary's conscience forces her to confess, only to learn that she's not the only cheater in the room.

♥ ***Raising Sweetness*** by Diane Stanley. Penguin Putnam, 2002. K–5. ALA Notable Children's Book. You'll be plumb tickled by this sequel to *Saving Sweetness* in which Tex, the big-hearted bachelor sheriff who adopted eight orphans, gets a letter from his long-lost sweetheart. 'Course he doesn't know it's from his long-lost sweetheart because neither he nor the children can read. Sweetheart eavesdrops on the evil schoolmistress and helps her unusual family grow in love and literacy. Sheer delight!

♥ ***Read for Me, Mama*** by Vashanti Rahaman. Boyds Mills Press, 1997. K–3. Joseph loves bringing books home from the school library. But when the neighbor who reads to him while Mama folds laundry goes away, Joseph discovers that Mama can't read. With help from Joseph and an adult literacy class, Mama overcomes her embarrassment and learns. What a victory when she finally shares Joseph's library books!

♥ ***Sixth Grade Can Really Kill You*** by Barthe DeClements. Penguin Putnam, 1994. 4–5. DeClements makes the link between poor school performance, poor self-image and poor behavior. Helen, who is dyslexic, is a sympathetic but not particularly lovable character. But students will relate to her and the honest portrayal of school culture. The author makes gradual progress toward a hopeful school future for Helen believable by deftly dealing with unhelpful parental attitudes and the strengths and limitations of school staff members.

♥ ***Spaceman*** by Jane Cutler. Dutton, 1997. 3–5. Gary has a terrible time in school and sometimes, to escape, simply "goes away" in his head. When he accidentally injures a classmate he is transferred to a special needs program. Everything is strange—the nontraditional classroom, the disorganized teacher and the unusual behavior of the students. Surprisingly, Gary begins to relax, make friends and, best of all, learn. A believable insight into the experience of a learning disabled student, full of engaging characters.

♥ ***The View from Saturday*** by E. L. Konigsburg. Simon & Schuster, 1998. 4–5. Newbery Medal Book, ALA Notable Children's Book. Sixth-grade teacher Mrs. Olinski, returning to teaching in a wheelchair after a disabling accident, must choose a class team for the Academic Bowl. Meanwhile four of her students are forging their own association based on unlikely connections and subtle similarities. This masterpiece of plot, characterization and message explores issues of character, intelligence, acceptance, confidence and learning.

♥ ***Wolf!*** by Becky Bloom. Orchard Books, 1999. K–5. When Wolf approaches the barnyard looking for lunch he is dismayed to be shooed away by animals that don't want to be distracted from their reading. He decides to learn to read himself, and perseveres until he impresses the farm animals by reading "with confidence and passion." As the book ends, the company of educated critters hit the road as a storytelling troupe! A delightful look at the joys of reading and storytelling.

♥ ***Zooman Sam*** by Lois Lowry. Random House, 2001. 2–4. It's career day at preschool and lovable Sam Krupnik goes as a zookeeper, complete with 30 hats representing animals he will tend! His costume is a hit; his teacher allows him time over a month to introduce his menagerie to the class. As Sam takes his teaching responsibilities seriously, he develops a new appreciation for teachers and also learns to read. Another rollicking Krupnik family adventure that celebrates learning and teaching.

Nonfiction

♥ ***Expanding Education & Literacy*** by Bernard Ryan Jr. Ferguson Publishing Company, 1998. 5+. This Community Service for Teens series title focuses on middle and high school students; some information and opportunities may not apply to elementary students. But it offers much basic information about what and how we learn and why literacy and education are important, as well as suggesting general approaches to service in this field, for mature elementary students. A good teacher resource as well.

♥ ***Illiteracy*** by Sean M. Grady. Gale Group, 1994. 5+. Another in the Lucent Overview series, this title explores the causes and costs of illiteracy and innumeracy in the U.S. and around the world. Startling statistics and subtle implications alert us to the seriousness of the problem, while a final chapter suggests the need for a broader understanding of the range of "basic skills" needed in today's complex society. Efforts to raise literacy rates are surveyed, along with an evaluation of challenges inherent in trying to bring basic skills to the world's diverse people.

♥ ***I'm New Here*** by Bud Howlett. Houghton Mifflin, 1993. 1–4. Jazmin Escalante is a recent immigrant from El Salvador who doesn't speak English. Howlett uses clear text and color photos to tell of Jazmin's difficult first week in her American school. With hope and without self-pity, Jazmin inspires readers to empathize with new students facing challenges of language and cultural adjustment.

♥ ***Just Kids: Visiting a Class for Children with Special Needs*** by Ellen B. Senisi. Dutton Children's Books, 1998. 1–3. Cindy is "sentenced" to visit a special education classroom after making an unkind remark on the playground. Over two weeks Cindy comes to know special needs children as individuals while learning about their particular challenges. While the book is rather text-heavy, the students are appealing and color photos make their stories feel real and personal. This title could be used effectively in sections, to introduce younger students to a variety of learning difficulties.

♥ *Learning is Fun with Mrs. Perez* by Alice K. Flanagan. Children's Press, 1998. K–2. Through minimal text, large type and color photos, young students see the creativity, dedication and home life of an exemplary kindergarten teacher. The book encourages students to notice and appreciate the efforts of their teachers.

♥ *Maria Montessori: Teacher of Teachers* by Marie Tennent Shephard. Lerner Publishing Group, 1996. 4–5. Shephard presents the life and career of this gifted, strong-willed physician-turned-educator who revolutionized theories of early childhood education around the world. In a balanced portrait, we see Dr. Montessori as a dedicated, compassionate and tireless advocate for children and also as a stubborn, controlling personality who was sometimes her own worst enemy. A challenging but worthwhile read for older students.

♥ *"Now I Get It!" 12 Ten-Minute Classroom Drama Skits for Science, Math, Language, and Social Studies, Volume I* by L. E. McCullough. Smith & Kraus, 2000. K–3. This teacher's resource book includes skits designed to consolidate learning in the title subjects by accommodating varied learning styles through drama. Simple skits with stage direction, prop suggestions and pre- and post-play activities offer a fun change of pace. Other "Now I Get It!" series titles address a variety of curriculum topics for these grades and for grades 4–6.

♥ *Succeeding with LD: 20 True Stories About Real People with LD* by Jill Lauren. Free Spirit Publishing, 1997. 4–5. Lauren introduces 20 people, ages 10 and up, with learning disabilities who have tackled their challenges with courage and determination. Each 4–7 page spread features black-and-white photos, quotes and best and worst school memories of one of the learners. The people are memorable; the writing is personal and engaging. An empathy-building introduction for older students.

Other Media

♥ *Smart Steps Fourth Grade* by DK Interactive Learning. Dorling Kidnersley, 2001 (CD-ROM). 4. This fun interactive CD offers 435 learning activities, tutorials and problems covering math, English and science subjects. It offers a reward system and individual progress tracking, using a friendly animated pencil guide and bright, appealing visuals. Look for other grade levels in the Smart Steps series.

♥ *The Wednesday Surprise* by Eve Bunting. Houghton Mifflin, 1991 (book and audiocassette). K–3. Anna and Grandma use their weekly baby-sitting time together to conspire over a birthday surprise for Anna's father. The reader is as delighted as Anna's father when the surprise is revealed—Anna has taught her grandmother to read! The child and adult narrators are very effective.

Web sites

♥ *Education Place Reading Scene*
www.eduplace.com/readingscene
This site offers an on-line book group for kids as well as games, quizzes and activities in the areas of reading, language arts, science, math and social studies.

♥ *Learning Disabilities OnLine*
www.ldonline.org/kidzone/

♥ *Seussville University*
www.seussville.com/seussville/university/
Fun activities in science, reasoning, math and reading for K–2 students.

♥ *The World of Reading*
www.worldreading.org

Service-Learning in Action

Here are some examples of service-learning projects in which elementary school students worked to support literacy and education.

♥ **Beech Street Buddies, Terre Haute, Indiana**

This project began in 1999 and has been continuously funded by grants from the Indiana Department of Education. Special Education teacher Pam McLin and then counselor Donna Wernz, of the Deming Elementary School, saw a need to build social, civic and academic skills in third to fifth grade students identified as at-risk or special needs. They contacted Tonya Williams, Director of the United Child Care Center in Terre Haute, about having Deming students make regular visits to the preschool with stories and activities. Williams was enthusiastic and has remained a staunch partner and supporter of the ongoing project. Students strengthen reading, math, social, civic and study skills as they choose appropriate books to share, prepare lesson plans including activities, determine and gather supplies, practice their reading and ultimately share their books and games with preschoolers in ways that boost the reading and school readiness of their young buddies. Monthly visits to the center begin in September and end with a picnic in May. Another Special Education teacher at Deming, Linda Johnson, now teams with McLin to oversee the project.

McLin and Johnson have watched students grow in all skill areas throughout the program years, as well as demonstrate positive character development and personal satisfaction at providing valuable assistance in the community. Both elementary and preschool students look forward to the visits, and participating preschoolers have experienced a smoother transition into kindergarten as a result of the extra attention from their older buddies. Everybody wins! To learn more about this successful project, contact:

Pam McLin
pkm@vigoschools.org

Linda Johnson
llj@vigoschools.org

Deming Elementary School
1750 8th Avenue
Terre Haute, IN 47807

♥ **"It's Cool to Start School" Video Project, Hanover, Indiana**

A brainstorming session with students in the Southwestern Jefferson County School District about how to improve children's perceptions of school produced the idea to team up elementary and high school students in producing a video introducing the school system to new kindergartners and their families. Students planned and developed the script and handled production and the necessary communications to create the video, which takes a lighthearted approach to welcoming new students. The video includes a visual tour of the school and commentaries on life at Southwestern Elementary. Then kindergarten teachers visited each student in his or her home to present the video. The video was produced in the spring of 2001 and presented in the fall of 2002. Participating teachers were Cindy Geisler, Shelly Anderson and Traci Ferguson. For more information contact:

Cindy Geisler
Southwestern Elementary School
273 Main Cross Street
Hanover, IN 47243
812-866-6205

Activities on Literacy and Education

Discussion Prompts

Use these prompts to stimulate discussion.

♥ **Importance of Reading.** Explore reasons why reading well is so important in our society. *Illiteracy, Expanding Education & Literacy* and *Succeeding with LD* address this subject.

- Why is it important to read well?

- What things would be hard for you to do if you couldn't read? Consider leisure-time activities as well as schoolwork.

- What things would be hard for your parents to do if they couldn't read well? Consider job-related tasks, shopping, getting around, managing a home and leisure-time activities.

♥ **Many Kinds of "Smart."** Many of the titles in this chapter bibliography feature characters who are smart in some ways and not in others. Share or assign one or more appropriate titles and then discuss using these questions.

- Do you think the main character in the book is smart? Why or why not? Is he or she smart in some ways and not in others?

- What does it mean to be smart? How can you tell if someone is smart? Is someone who doesn't speak English well, who gets poor grades or who learns slowly less intelligent than others?

- Is anyone good at everything? Is anyone bad at everything? Do you think most people are smart in some ways and not in others?

- Is it smart to understand what things you're good and poor at, and to ask for help to improve in your weak areas?

- Do the characters in the books recognize their learning challenges and seek help? Why or why not?

♥ **Informal Education.** Learning happens both inside and outside of school, as depicted in *Just Juice, Fourth Grade Weirdo, Barry* and *The View from Saturday.* Consider these questions about out of school, nonacademic learning.

- Who has taught you something valuable outside of school?

- What did this person teach you? Why is it valuable to you?

- How did this person teach and how did you learn?

♥ **Obstacles to Learning.** *Jake Drake Teacher's Pet, Mary Marony and the Chocolate Surprise, Just Juice* and *Aunt Chip and the Great Triple Creek Dam Affair* all involve things (other than learning disabilities) that get in the way of learning. Use one or more of them to begin to explore some of the obstacles to learning (e.g., cheating, too much competition, criticism or favoritism).

- What things make it hard to learn in the classroom? Outside the classroom?

- How do these obstacles get in the way of learning?

- What can you do if one of these obstacles is making it hard for you to learn?

Games

♥ **Word Scramble.** Enjoy the word scramble puzzle on page 83, using words and phrases that relate to literacy, education and learning.

♥ **Flashcard Bingo.** Create bingo cards featuring letters or numbers for each student (see examples on page 84). Use the cards to make a game of drilling basic information like matching letters to sounds, spelling words or simple math facts. You might work orally from your own lists with the whole class or use this as a learning center game and have students drill each other using their Personal Flash Cards (below). Use pennies, tiddlywinks disks or other markers to cover the called squares. When students get "bingo," they might receive a small prize.

Creative Expressions

Enjoy these creative ways to process concepts from the books on the list.

♥ **Personal Flash Cards.** Have students cut out and decorate sets of at least 26 4" x 6" blank flashcards from tagboard. Students should decorate the borders and leave the centers of the cards blank. Laminate the cards so they can be written on with wipe-off crayons, overhead markers or wax pens and used repeatedly to drill letters or words, numbers, simple math problems or science or history facts. Use the cards with Flashcard Bingo on page 78.

♥ **Teaching and Learning Essays.** Have students write two essays. The first should explain "How ___ helped me learn to…" and the second, "How I helped ____ learn to…." Students might share one of their essays aloud.

♥ **Appreciating Teachers.** Using basic craft materials, have students make a card or small gift to give to a favorite teacher in appreciation of his or her skills and assistance.

♥ **Expressive Reading.** Read *Wolf!* aloud. Have students find a short story they enjoy and practice until they can read or tell the story to the class "with confidence and passion." Have fun sharing stories!

Research Opportunities

♥ **Local Literacy Programs.** Research literacy programs available in the local community. Who operates them? Who and how many students do they serve? Are there statistics on how many residents of the community are totally or functionally illiterate? What are their needs? Share findings as a class and start to think about how you might assist these organizations. Use the resources on page 80.

♥ **Favorite Teachers.** Interview a favorite teacher about his or her life, education and career. Then tell the class about your favorite teacher, explaining why you chose that person. You might extend this activity by inviting the teachers to a reception in their honor, where students can introduce them in person.

♥ **Social Promotion.** Find out about your school district's policies on social promotion (advancing students from grade to grade based on age rather than skill levels) and how they have changed over time. Then discuss or debate whether social promotion is a good or bad idea.

♥ **Learning Disabilities.** Using *Just Kids* and *Succeeding with LD* as starting points, have interested students study a particular learning disability and report to the class on what's known about it and ways of addressing it. A particularly interesting topic to explore is Irlen Syndrome, also called Scotopic Sensitivity Syndrome. Information can be found at: www.irlen.com/sss_main.htm.

Miscellaneous Activities

♥ **Montessori Method.** Is there a Montessori school in your community? Have older students read *Maria Montessori*. Then visit a Montessori school and observe her methods in action. Meet with a staff member to ask how teachers are trained, how students learn and how effective the method is at teaching traditional subjects and practical life skills.

♥ **Skills Swap.** In *Barry,* Barry and Woodsie "swap skills." Barry coaches Woodsie in hockey strategies and Woodsie helps Barry with math concepts. Create your own in-class skills swap by having each student identify something he or she does well and create a simple lesson plan to teach it to a classmate. Use the worksheet on page 82 to help students plan. Then randomly pair up students to swap roles, executing their lesson plans. You might also review the lesson plans and assign partners based on your knowledge of your students. Or give students a list of skills without identifying names. Let them indicate several choices in priority order, then assign to accommodate interests as best you can. Each student should experience being both learner and teacher.

♥ **The Perfect Teacher.** Throughout this chapter you might invite students to share their thoughts about what makes a good teacher. Display a poster with a figure of a person labeled "The Perfect Teacher." As they process ideas about teaching and learning, students may write words or phrases on the poster that describe a good teacher. They might list qualities like "patient" or "funny," or behaviors like "doesn't play favorites."

♥ **It's Greek to Me!** Is there a teacher in your school who is fluent in another language? Invite that teacher to enter your classroom and begin to instruct students in a language other than English, with no prior explanation. Continue for several minutes and watch class reaction. When the class is sufficiently confused or frustrated, shift into discussion mode aimed at sensitizing students to the experience of non-English speaking immigrant children starting school in America. Talk about how it feels to not understand, and what it does and doesn't mean about their intelligence and abilities. Consider how much stronger those feelings might be if you were the only one who didn't understand. Use *I'm New Here* to consolidate the concepts.

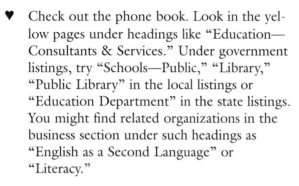

In Your Community

Use these starting points to discover needs and activity in your local community.

♥ Check out the phone book. Look in the yellow pages under headings like "Education—Consultants & Services." Under government listings, try "Schools—Public," "Library," "Public Library" in the local listings or "Education Department" in the state listings. You might find related organizations in the business section under such headings as "English as a Second Language" or "Literacy."

♥ Call your city hall or county supervisor's office and ask what agencies work with literacy or education issues and what community organizations help.

♥ Check out SERVEnet (www.servenet.org) to see what organizations are addressing these issues in your area. Two other Web sites, Family Literacy Program Directory (www.famlit.org/famlitnetwork/) and America's Literacy Directory (www.literacydirectory.org) can also help you locate nearby programs.

♥ Watch local newspapers and other publications for articles related to literacy and lifelong learning.

♥ Talk to people "in the know" on these subjects. They might be state government officials, school board members, members of ethnic or cultural organizations, public librarians, private tutors or representatives of literacy programs such as Literacy Volunteers of America or Laubach Literacy International. Invite resource people to visit the class or assign students to interview them and report back. Find out what they think are the greatest obstacles to having a literate, well-educated local population.

Taking Action

Based on your research about literacy and education issues in your community, plan a service-learning project. These ideas might help you start generating suggestions.

♥ Check out the Reading is Fundamental Web site and consider participating in the "Books on the Menu" program as a class. Find it at: www.rif.org/programs/speclitprgs/booksmenu.html.

♥ Create a picture book or set of picture books to give to new kindergarten students welcoming them to the school.

♥ Develop a student-driven "Teacher of the Month" display to recognize and appreciate the efforts of good teachers.

♥ Create a plan to welcome new students to your class. Test it on a new student or two, refine it and then propose it to the whole school. This effort could evolve into a school-wide welcome club for new students.

♥ Set core information to music to help younger students memorize things like multiplication tables, names of states, U.S. presidents, etc. You might enlist the help of a music teacher and arrange for students to teach their songs to appropriate grades.

♥ Organize an Academic Bowl, as in *The View from Saturday,* to review core knowledge within your grade or school. This can be done in different ways to emphasize either cooperation or competition.

♥ Raise funds to support a local literacy or ESL program. Consider an event that uses basic skills practice, such as a read-a-thon, as the means for raising funds.

♥ Donate books to homeless shelters or agencies that help low-income children, who may not have books of their own.

 **More Ideas**

Suggest these ideas to motivated students who want to help as individuals.

♥ Seek your parents' help to volunteer as a conversation or reading buddy for a special needs student, ESL student or international high school exchange student.

♥ Volunteer time as a peer tutor or homework helper for a special needs student in your class or school. Resources like Smart Steps software in the chapter bibliography might be useful.

♥ Make a personal commitment to help welcome new students to your school and to befriend students who are being treated unkindly because of learning or language challenges.

♥ If you're too young to serve as a tutor in a local literacy or ESL program, help out in other ways such as set-up before or clean-up after classes, fund-raising or promotional campaigns.

♥ Keep learning about the issues and expressing your informed views to your local paper, local government officials and national politicians.

Skills Swap Lesson Plan

Think of something you do well. Use this worksheet to create a lesson plan to teach your particular skill to a classmate. Let your teacher help you decide the right "size" skill or task to teach.

My skill or talent: _____

The specific thing I will teach: _____

I will use these methods to teach:

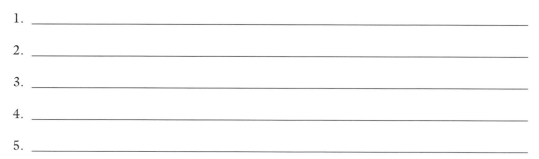

- ☐ Tell about it in words (lecture)

- ☐ Talk about it with my "student" (discuss)

- ☐ Show examples of the product (display)

- ☐ Show how it's done (demonstrate)

- ☐ Have my "student" practice with me (model)

- ☐ Have my "student" practice while I watch (supervise)

- ☐ Have my "student" do the task independently (evaluate)

- ☐ Other _____

I will need these materials: _____

_____

_____

Here is my step-by-step lesson plan:

1. _____

2. _____

3. _____

4. _____

5. _____

Here's how I'll know my "student" learned what I wanted to teach:

_____

_____

_____

Literacy and Learning Word Scramble

Draw a line from the scrambled words and phrases in the first column to their unscrambled versions in the second column. See the clues at the bottom of the page.

1.	USEORECR OMOR	TUTOR
2.	TYERILAC	SECOND LANGUAGE
3.	ROUTT	LEARNING DISORDER
4.	DACONETUI	EDUCATION
5.	NERLA	TEACHER
6.	RINNGLAE DROSERDI	DYSLEXIA
7.	RETHECA	RESOURCE ROOM
8.	NANYMIUREC	INNUMERACY
9.	DOSNEC ENAGLUGA	LITERACY
10.	YADSEXIL	LEARN

Clues

1. Where students go to get extra help at school.

2. The ability to read and write.

3. A person who gives individual help to a learner.

4. What you go to school to get.

5. What you go to school to do.

6. When someone has trouble reading or remembering, he or she may have a ____ ____.

7. A person who is trained to help you learn is a _____.

8. The inability to read numbers or do simple math problems.

9. Many immigrants must take English as a ____ ____ classes.

10. A common learning disorder.

Letter and Number Bingo Cards

Use these samples to create bingo cards for reviewing basic letter, word or math facts. You'll need sets of unique cards in order to make a game for the entire class. Simply use the random patterns below offset by one square for each card to make as many cards as you need for your class. For example, make the second letter bingo card with squares starting from the top left and reading "F, Q, B, A, I" and add "O" to the bottom right of the card. A blank card to copy is located on page 85.

O	F	Q	B	A	I
Y	W	O	U	H	O
G	A	L	R	I	M
U	I	P	E	C	V
N	K	E	E	J	A
Z	D	U	T	S	X

3	20	1	15	7	19
24	29	11	33	26	27
8	2	32	23	18	16
10	14	34	13	4	31
21	36	28	5	22	35
25	6	30	17	12	9

Note: Keeping the letters or numbers in the corners of the squares allows students to mark the squares without covering them for future words or problems. Tell students to stack additional markers on letters or numbers that are used more than once in a game.

Blank Bingo Card

Promoting Justice

In a sense this chapter serves as an overview or culmination of earlier chapters, since each issue area that might be addressed through service-learning projects is grounded in the concept of justice. Whether we concern ourselves with the needs of the hungry, the humane treatment of animals or protecting the environment, what we're really talking about is understanding what is fair and right and providing "justice for all" in the present and into the future.

The Merriam-Webster's Collegiate Dictionary describes justice as determining and maintaining rights based on rules of law and equity. The word justice, for most of us, connotes fair resolution of conflicts, impartiality, sharing of resources, equal opportunities, protection of rights, prosecution of criminals and restitution for victims. What does justice look like in action? We might envision people working together in an atmosphere of peace and security to provide basic needs, protect basic rights and offer hope for some level of personal fulfillment for every individual. In a just society each person could contribute his or her best to our collective safety, well-being and richness of opportunities. Idealistic? Definitely. Yet some form of this vision persists as the loftiest hope and dream for most people. Whether we're fighting the ill effects of favoritism in the classroom, bullying on the playground, hunger and poverty, violent street crime or terrorism around the world, justice seems to be the key.

How can we encourage students to think about and actively promote justice in their lives and the world? These ideas might help focus your exploration of this broad and complex subject.

♥ Defining "basic rights"—The Universal Declaration of Human Rights and the UN Convention on the Rights of the Child.

♥ Valuing others as highly as ourselves and the role of empathy.

♥ Sharing protection, resources and opportunities fairly—legal, economic and social justice.

♥ Nonviolent conflict resolution/mediation.

♥ Peace as a by-product of justice.

♥ Different approaches to justice—e.g., "An Eye for an Eye" vs. The Golden Rule.

♥ The need for laws and law enforcement to protect our rights with impartiality.

♥ Preventing and fighting crime.

Resources on Promoting Justice

Use these resources to build knowledge and stimulate involvement in issues of promoting justice.

Fiction

♥ **Cam Jansen and the Mystery at the Haunted House** by David A. Adler. Penguin Putnam, 1999. 2–4. Spunky fifth grader Cam and her photographic memory are back to solve the case of the amusement park purse snatcher in this easy chapter book. While few children share this likable character's special crime-busting skill, all can cheer her on and enjoy her success.

♥ **The Case of the Goblin Pearls** by Laurence Yep. HarperCollins, 1998. 3–5. Set in San Francisco's Chinatown, this mystery pits young Lily and her flamboyant actress-detective-aunt against a street gang and a pair of unscrupulous high-society thieves trying to build an empire on the backs of abused sweatshop workers. The hilarity of Aunt Tiger Lil's schemes and the chaos of the Chinese New Year contrast with the dismal portrayal of sweatshop conditions and grinding poverty.

♥ **The Cow of No Color** by Nina Jaffe and Steve Zeitlin. Henry Holt and Company, 1998. K–5. Jaffe and Zeitlin provide a wonderful collection of stories from around the world that challenge us to ponder what is just and fair. Some are presented as riddles and invite reflection. They may be used individually, as teasers or discussion starters or assigned as a package to older readers. You might read and discuss one story each day that you work on this chapter.

♥ **Don't Tell Anyone** by Peg Kehret. Penguin Putnam, 2002. 3–5. Twelve-year-old Megan is at the center of converging plots in this suspenseful novel, due to her concern for a group of wild cats living in a field. When she learns the field is to be cleared for construction she tries to save the animals, unwittingly disrupting the plans of a dangerous criminal. In the process she becomes the only witness to a hit-and-run accident. Along with obvious issues of animal welfare and criminal justice, a subtler issue emerges as the hit-and-run driver struggles with her conscience and learns about being fair to herself.

♥ **Frindle** by Andrew Clements. Simon & Schuster, 1997. 2–5. When bright, unconventional Nick's equally unconventional fifth grade teacher gets him thinking about where words come from he tries an experiment, replacing the word "pen" with his creation, "frindle." It catches on! But Mrs. Granger values rules and order and resists the growing lexicological movement. The zany conflict attracts national media as a freedom of speech issue, putting both Nick and Mrs. Granger in spotlights they didn't intend. This funny, heartwarming story takes a fresh look at freedom, rights and the positive potential of conflict. A winner!

♥ **Matilda** by Roald Dahl. Penguin USA, 1998. 3–5. Although presenting a decidedly "kid's eye view" of justice, there is much to enjoy and explore in this darkly funny fantasy about a gifted girl whose low-life parents neglect her and whose school headmistress terrorizes her and her schoolmates. Injustice triggers Matilda's anger, which in turn triggers psychokinetic powers that she uses to get back at her tormentors. In true fairy tale style, a kind teacher and good friends help Matilda vanquish evil in her world and reach a happy ending.

♥ **The Moon Over Crete** by Jyotsna Sreenivasan. Smooth Stone Press, 1997. 3–5. In this unusual time-travel story Lily is transported to ancient Crete, where she experiences a culture in which women and men work together with mutual respect and equality. The experience helps Lily deal with issues of gender stereotypes and sexual harassment in her everyday life. An endnote explains the basis of the author's vision of ancient Cretan society.

♥ **Nabulela** by Fiona Moodie. Farrar, Straus and Giroux, 1997. K–3. Sea monster Nabulela is terrorizing the people of an African village. When the village girls are unfair and cruel to the favored daughter of the tribal chief, they are charged to kill Nabulela to atone for their injustice. Not only do they succeed but the chief also recognizes his unfairness in spoiling his daughter. This old tale satisfies the reader with a sense of justice served.

♥ **Peace Begins with You** by Katherine Scholes. Little, Brown and Company, 1994. K–5. Scholes looks at what peace means to people, the basic elements needed to ensure peace for everyone and obstacles to peace. Soft, warm illustrations reinforce the personal, caring messages of this introduction to the topic.

♥ **Serial Sneak Thief** by E. W. Hildick. Marshall Cavendish, 1997. 3–5. What kid wouldn't love a creative children's librarian who used to be a detective? In this Felicity Snell Mystery, the popular librarian's Mystery Club game (follow the clues and crack the case of "the body in the library") heats up into some real-life sleuthing for Junior Detectives as a vengeful thief goes after valuable library treasures. Will justice be done?

♥ **Shadow Dance** by Donna Perrone and Tololwa M. Mollel. Houghton Mifflin, 1998. K–5. Salome saves a crocodile trapped in the weeds, only to be captured by the ungrateful animal for lunch. Salome argues for justice, but several "impartial" parties refuse to help. Finally she finds a friend who helps her beat the crocodile at his own game. A good look at "a taste of your own medicine" justice.

♥ **Two Fine Ladies Have a Tiff** by Antonia Zehler. Random House, 2002. K–1. In this beginning reader two friends have a disagreement that turns into a fight. The simple, sweet outcome implies that conflict resolution sometimes involves forgiving and forgetting, rather than solving the specific problems at hand.

Nonfiction

♥ **Crime Detection** by Chris Oxlade. Heinemann Library, 1997. 3–5. This fascinating book should appeal to students interested in science or the mystery genre. It introduces aspects of science used in preventing and solving crimes, from security systems to forensic medicine. Appealing layout and colorful illustrations invite sampling. A good starting point for research into science in service of justice.

♥ **Every Kid's Guide to Handling Family Arguments** by Joy Berry. Children's Press, 1991. 3–5. Illustrated in bright cartoon style and featuring a cartoon family, this Living Skills series title examines the inevitability and causes of family arguments. Berry maintains that arguments can be good or bad, and gives step-by-step suggestions for handling them positively and guidelines for avoiding unnecessary conflict. The family dog's reactions to events add humor. Another useful title in this series is *Every Kid's Guide to Handling Disagreements*.

♥ **For Every Child: The UN Convention on the Rights of the Child in Words and Pictures** by Caroline Castle. Phyllis Fogelman Books, 2001. K–5. This lovely picture book features illustrations by well-known children's illustrators, depicting the spirit of specific rights of children as adopted by the UN in 1989. A powerful tool for introducing the idea that justice must be founded on an understanding of shared basic rights.

♥ **In RE: Gault (1967): Juvenile Justice** by Susan Dudley Gold. Millbrook Press, 1995. 5+. While stretching the limits for most readers in this age range, this volume in the Supreme Court Decision series provides a detailed look at the history of juvenile justice and a case that provided important legal protection for all children in America. Through this landmark decision children were granted many constitutional rights to due process of law formerly denied them. Much food for thought, discussion and research.

♥ **Journey to the Soviet Union** by Samantha Smith. Little, Brown and Company, 1985. 3–5. Much has changed since this book's release— the Soviet Union is no more, Samantha Smith died in a plane crash and the book went out of print! But it is available in many libraries and effectively shares, in photos and Smith's words, the story of this charming young peace activist who attracted world attention at age 10 with her letter to then-president of the Soviet Union Yuri Andropov, and his response. An inspiration. Students might research what has come of Smith's experiences over the years since her famous letter, her travels and her untimely death.

♥ **Laws** by Zachary A. Kelly. Rourke Publishing, 1999. K–5. This Law and Order series title looks at legal justice in terms of deciding who was wrong and who was wronged, punishing the guilty and repaying the victim. It explains why we have laws and how they are made and enforced at local, state and federal levels. Kelly delivers an admirable amount of substance in a slim, inviting picture book. The *Law Enforcement* title from the same series may also be useful.

♥ **Peace on the Playground: Nonviolent Ways of Problem-Solving** by Eileen Lucas. Franklin Watts, 1991. 3–5. Lucas explores the role of conflict in our lives and makes the case for seeking peaceful resolution. She offers nonviolent strategies for different issues and settings. Along the way she honors such peacemakers as Gandhi, Samantha Smith and Desmond Tutu. A good primer on seeking justice and making peace.

● ***Police Officers*** by Paulette Bourgeois. Kids Can Press, 2000. K–3. This title from the In My Neighborhood series uses a loose plot to introduce the role of a local patrol officer and goes on to explore other law enforcement jobs. It shows a child helping officers solve a crime through observation and reporting, and encourages personal safety.

● ***Stand up for Your Rights: A Book About Human Rights Written by and for the Young People of the World***, edited by Peace Child International. World Book, Inc., 2000. 4–5. This volume celebrates the 50th anniversary of the Universal Declaration of Human Rights. Using illustrations, poems, diary entries and personal reflections by children around the world, the book presents the articles of the declaration in plain language and explores examples of their application and abuse since their adoption. Concepts are complex and events described are sometimes intense but the balanced, hopeful tone makes the book well worth sharing with older students.

● ***The United Nations*** by Ann Armbruster. Franklin Watts, 1997. 2–5. Nicely illustrated with photographs, this title traces the world's "only international organization dedicated to peace, justice and economic equality" from its inception to the near-present. It honestly presents the UN's great successes, struggles and failures and the uneven support of its members, as well as its potential for effectiveness in a rapidly changing world.

● ***Women of Peace: Nobel Peace Prize Winners*** by Anne Schraff. Enslow Publishers, 1994. 3–5. This Collective Biographies title makes a clear connection between peace and justice through the stories of nine women awarded the Nobel Peace Prize between 1905 and 1994. Clearly written and accessible, it's an excellent introduction to these exceptional women.

Other Media

● ***Brother Future*** by Roy Campanella II. Goldhil Home Media, 1991 (videocassette). 3–5. T. J. is an irresponsible, streetwise African American teen whose business, fencing stolen goods, takes precedence over school. An injury catapults him back in time to pre-Civil War South Carolina where he experiences the life of a plantation slave and gains a new perspective on priorities, values and justice. This sometimes-violent WonderWorks Family Movie effectively suggests the abomination of slavery and provides a view of American society as moving slowly along the very long path from gross injustice to full equality.

● ***Golden Rule*** designed by Jeffrey Streiff. Special Ideas, 1991 (poster). K–5. This poster shows five children from different cultures praying in different ways, illustrating expressions of the Golden Rule from Buddhist, Jewish, Christian, Muslim and Baha'i scriptures. A nice way to emphasize the primacy of this approach to justice across times, places and religions. Available through Special Ideas (www.special-ideas.com).

● ***Teaching Peace*** by Red Grammer. Smilin' Atcha Music, 1986 (audiocassette). K–2. This award-winning cassette includes fun, catchy songs for younger children about self-esteem, praising others, solving problems with words, listening and celebrating diversity. Great for background, or use specific songs to illustrate justice-related concepts or stimulate discussion.

Web sites

● ***Iowa Department of Public Safety Kids Page***
www.state.ia.us/government/dps/kids/
Invites kids to become junior DEI agents through games and activities.

● ***Justice for Kids & Youth***
www.usdoj.gov/kidspage/
Sections for K–5 include "Civil Rights," "Inside the Courtroom" and "FBI."

● ***One World, Many Rights—A Celebration of Human Rights and the Rights of the Child***
www.occdsb.on.ca/~sel/rights/rights.htm

● ***People for Peace/Kids for Peace***
members.aol.com/pforpeace/WorkItOut/

● ***UNICEF Voices of Youth***
www.unicef.org/voy/

Here are examples of service-learning involving elementary students with issues of justice in their communities.

♥ **The Bus Bully Project, North Adams, Massachusetts**

Like most school districts, North Adams had a problem with bullying and chaotic behavior on school buses. In the fall of 1999 Brayton Elementary third grade teacher Karen Lefave noticed that unpleasant bus experiences could set a negative tone for a student's whole day. She talked with school counselor Nancy Gallagher and the two decided to approach Lefave's class about tackling the problem as a service-learning initiative. They agreed! The class developed a plan that involved language arts, science, art and social skills. Students conducted a pre-project survey. Then they spent a week documenting problem behavior on buses. Considering their data, they decided to focus on bullying. They brainstormed ways to address the problem, expressed their feelings through art and creative writing, kept journals and role-played. They quickly discovered that many of the bullies were older students and decided to enlist the help of fifth graders in understanding and reducing bullying behavior. Groups of third and fifth graders (with cooperation from fifth grade teacher Madeline Carlow) discussed bullying, did role-plays and took a "bully test" to examine their own behavior for bullying tendencies. They practiced strategies for saying "no" to bullies. At year's end students invited bus drivers and school and town officials to a "bullyproofing presentation" to share their accomplishments. A post-project survey showed evidence of improvement in the bus situation and a legacy of aware and empowered students.

In the second year students decided that contributing factors to bus chaos were a lack of relationship with bus drivers and an unclear understanding of bus rules. They added two elements to the program. They rewrote the district's bus rules in kid-friendly language for distribution throughout the school. And they planned a process of interviewing bus drivers, making posters about them, getting to know them and expressing appreciation for them. Again, results were positive. Victims of bullies gained understanding and strategies to protect themselves. Older students gained awareness of the damage and dangers of bullying behavior to themselves and others. Bus drivers and riders gained a sense of community responsibility for each other. And Lefave's students showed potential as emerging social activists, ready to take on the world! For more information contact:

Debbie Coyne
Service-Learning Coordinator for the North Adams School District
413-662-3240
coyneds@hotmail.com.

♥ **Conflict Managers/Conflict Coaches, Dallas Center-Grimes School District, Iowa**

Over a decade, guidance counselors and teachers at Dallas Center-Grimes Elementary School developed a "homegrown" peer conflict management program based on research into national concepts and models. Teachers were trained in conflict management strategies and decided to pass on their training in a service-learning mode to selected students from each third-fifth grade classroom. For the first several years, chosen "Conflict Managers" completed an orientation along with their parents, followed by a day-long training session and regular after-school training covering active listening, handling emotions, talking about feelings, problem clarification, generating fair solutions, objectivity and consensus building. Training involved discussion, role-playing, puppet skits, creative writing and visual art projects. Conflict Managers served during recess, to help settle playground conflicts, or worked with in-building referrals.

Later, encouraged by successes, staff decided to make conflict management training available to all students, using trained classroom representatives, called Conflict Coaches, to take skills training back to their classes. They also decided to include second graders.

As part of the program Dallas Center-Grimes students performed skits on conflict resolution for community groups and presented the program at a statewide Peace Conference. In 1997 they received a Governor's Volunteer Award. Parents reported carryover of conflict resolution strategies at home, and students took pride in their ability to manage their lives better and to help others find fair solutions to conflict. For more information contact:

Jill Pickell
515-992-3838
pickell@netins.net

Discussion Prompts

Use these prompts to explore issues of rights and justice.

♥ **Understanding Rights.** While justice is a big concept involving many aspects, it clearly involves defining and protecting basic rights to which we should feel entitled. Several books in this chapter deal with rights, including *For Every Child, Stand up for Your Rights, In RE: Gault (1967)* and *Women of Peace.* Using these books as starting points, discuss the rights we have defined as basic for citizens of the U.S. or of the world:

- What do we mean by civil rights? Human rights? The rights of children?

- How are these lists of rights similar? How are they different?

- What things do we currently do to try to protect these basic rights?

- What more could we do to protect these basic rights for every American? For every citizen of the world?

♥ **Kinds of Justice.** It helps to understand the concept of justice to analyze it in categories. *Laws* looks at elements of legal justice. *For Every Child* and *Stand up for Your Rights* address areas of social justice, involving values and attitudes as well as laws and economics. Review these titles and invite the class to create lists of examples of justice or injustice in action for each category.

♥ **Conflict Resolution.** Conflicts happen because people have different ideas, wants and opinions. But there are many ways of responding to conflicts. Several books in this chapter discuss resolving everyday conflicts, including *Peace Begins with You, Every Kid's Guide to Handling Family Arguments* and *Peace on the Playground.* Assign one or more of the titles on this subject as preparation. Then read aloud or review *Two Fine Ladies Have a Tiff* and *Shadow Dance.* Discuss their different approaches to conflict resolution:

- How does Salome resolve her conflict with the crocodile in *Shadow Dance*? How do the Two Fine Ladies settle their tiff?

- Salome's approach to justice is to beat the crocodile at his own game—a "taste of your own medicine" approach. The Fine Ladies don't really solve the disagreements at all. Their approach is more about the Golden Rule, or "forgiving and forgetting." Do both approaches serve justice? How are they similar and different?

- Which is harder to do—respond to unfairness by being equally unfair or to treat others the way you'd like to be treated? Why?

- Which approach might be more effective in teaching fairness and justice? Does it depend on the situation? Why?

Note: With older students, you might lead a similar discussion based on stories from The Cow of No Color, Frindle, Matilda *or other books from the bibliography.* Matilda *offers an opportunity to discuss revenge as a response to injustice.*

Games

♥ **Encoded Message Puzzle.** Use the reproducible puzzle sheet on page 95 to test students' decoding skills and decipher a message about justice. The message: "Justice means protecting everyone's rights and treating people equally."

♥ **Crime-Stopper Charades.** *Police Officers* includes tips for preventing crime and examples of kids helping to catch criminals. Read the book together. Then divide the class into teams of 3–4 students. Explain basic charades procedures, like indicating the number of syllables in a word, specifying a word in a phrase, "sounds like" and "looks like" gestures, etc. Hand each team a card with a phrase related to preventing or solving crime. Give teams a few minutes to plan their strategies. Teams should start by trying to act out their phrase for the class. Then one member will signal specific words. Give each team 3 minutes to convey their phrase while the rest of the class tries to guess it. If it is correctly identified in time the presenting team gets one point and the person who guesses the phrase earns one point for his or her team. Here are some sample phrases:

- Call 9-1-1.

- Don't confront criminals!

- Watch closely, remember details.
- Don't touch evidence!
- Walk with a buddy.
- Lock your doors.
- Have a family password.
- Register your bicycle.
- Report suspicious behavior.

♥ **Where Do You Stand?** This game gets students moving and thinking about acting on behalf of justice. Start with four different-colored sheets of poster board. Mark the sheets "1," "2," "3" and "4." Line them up on the floor. Then present a series of scenarios with 4 possible responses. For example, you might say, "You find out that the company that makes your favorite snack food uses child labor and unfair labor practices. Should you: 1) Write a letter to the president of the company protesting and keep buying the snack? 2) Stop buying the snack and write a letter to the company protesting and telling them about your personal boycott? 3) Organize your friends to boycott the snack and picket local stores that sell it? 4) Keep buying the snack because your efforts won't change anything anyway?" As you read the choices, students line up behind the sheet related to the choice they like best. Students may change lines as you give more options. But in the end they must choose a line and be able to explain why. There don't always have to be clear "right" and "wrong" choices. Discuss which responses most children choose and why. You might assign students to write scenarios to use in playing the game, after demonstrating how it is played with one or two examples. Then play using appropriate student-generated situations.

Creative Expressions

Enjoy these creative ways to process concepts from books on the list.

♥ **Illustrating the Rights of the Child**. Share *For Every Child* with the class. Explain how the illustrations go with specific rights adopted by the UN. Place the book at a learning center with basic art supplies. Have students choose an article from the back of the book, read the description and create an illustration expressing that article as the book's illustrators did. Illustrations might be collected and arranged to create a classroom collage about children's rights.

♥ **Creative Writing Challenge.** Challenge older students to a similar process by introducing *Stand up for Your Rights* and explaining its format. Have students choose one of the Articles from the Universal Declaration of Human Rights, study the appropriate spread in the book and create a poem, essay or journal entry expressing their thoughts.

♥ **Magic Justice Machines.** After reading and discussing concepts from this chapter invite students to design a "magic justice machine" to help them carry out their dreams, hopes and wishes for justice in the world. You might provide supplies to build models of their designs or simply have them design on paper. This is an exercise of imagination; students are free to fantasize without considering practicality or reality. Have them share their designs. What do they look like? What can they do?

Research Opportunities

♥ **Local Crime Prevention.** Find out about crime prevention programs operating in your community. Start with your local police department. Are there Neighborhood Watch programs? D.A.R.E. programs? Ask how kids can be involved in starting or supporting such programs.

♥ **Federal Law Enforcement.** Research federal law enforcement agencies like the U.S. Marshals, FBI and INS. What role does each play in preventing or solving crimes? In protecting rights? In upholding justice? Have students prepare reports for the class including charts, photographs or other visual elements.

♥ **The United Nations.** Use the reproducible worksheet on page 96 to guide students in learning about the only global organization dedicated to peace, justice and equal rights for all the world's people. Use *The United Nations* as a starting point.

♥ **Forensic Science.** Invite interested students to study one of the scientific techniques introduced in *Crime Detection,* used to prevent or solve crimes. If possible, have students share their knowledge in demonstration form.

Miscellaneous Activities

♥ **Free Speech for Kids.** Talk about children's right to speak out about injustice around them and discuss how students currently do or don't practice that right. Then divide the class into small groups and assign each to choose an issue of justice or injustice in their lives that they want to speak up about. Once each group has chosen an issue, each student will write a "letter to the editor" composition about the group's issue. Compile the compositions into a newsletter and print it for distribution around school. This activity could evolve into an ongoing display of kids speaking out about different issues each month. Younger students might record their thoughts about an issue on audiocassette, to be transcribed for sharing.

♥ **Chains of Injustice.** This two-part activity explores examples of injustice that symbolically bind us in chains and examples of justice that free us. First, cut construction paper into 1" strips the short way, so each strip is 1" x 9". Give each student a strip. Go around the room, having each student suggest a form of injustice in a word or short phrase. They might suggest things like racism or child labor, or more immediate issues like "First graders get to eat lunch before fifth graders." As students share their examples they should write them on their strips of paper and pass them to you to be joined together into a paper chain using staples. When the chain is complete with a link from each student, talk about how injustice restricts our freedom and holds us back, like a chain. Second, go back through the chain, link by link. Read each injustice and have the class suggest a way to resolve the conflict or make the wrong right. As an idea emerges to address each injustice, use scissors to cut that link off the chain.

♥ **Book Reports.** Have students read fiction titles from the chapter bibliography and write book reports including these items:

- summary of the story

- what the story has to say about justice

- if you would recommend the book, and why or why not

♥ **Court in Action.** Invite an officer of family, juvenile or peer court to visit the class; or arrange a field trip to tour the courthouse and observe family, juvenile or peer court in session.

In Your Community

Use these starting points to discover needs and activity in your community.

♥ Check out the phone book. Look in the yellow pages under headings like "Mediation Services" or "Legal Services." Check government listings under "Law Enforcement" or, in county listings, "Court Services," "Family Violence," "Peer Court," "Juvenile Court" or "Legal Aid Society." At the state level, try "Department of Human Rights," "Citizens Aide Ombudsman," "Civil Rights Commission," "Criminal Investigation Bureau," "Criminal & Juvenile Justice" or "Attorney General." You might have a Better Business Bureau, which deals with consumer rights, in your community.

♥ Call your city hall or county supervisor's office and ask what agencies work with aspects of justice and what community organizations help.

♥ Search SERVEnet (www.servenet.org) for organizations that advocate for rights and justice in your area.

♥ Watch the local newspapers and other publications for articles on how your community seeks to protect rights and uphold justice.

♥ Talk to people "in the know" on this subject. They might be government employees, like juvenile or family court judges, or members of organizations like Human Rights Watch, Amnesty International or the NAACP. Find out what problems of legal, economic or social injustice these people see and what they think are the greatest needs in the community.

Taking Action

Based on your research, develop a plan for your service-learning project. These ideas might get you started.

♥ Sponsor representatives from your school to go through the Anti-Defamation League's World of Difference Peer Leadership Program (www.adl.org/awod_new/awod_peer_lead.asp) or the Educators for Social Responsibility's

Resolving Conflict Creatively Program Peer Mediation training (www.esrnational.org/about-rccp.html).

♥ Work with local police to set up a Neighborhood Watch program for the school's neighborhood.

♥ Raise money to help support a local organization that works to protect people's rights and promote justice in your town.

♥ Design a community-wide survey to take nominations for a citizen who has done the most to promote justice locally. Determine the winner and plan a school assembly, with the public invited, to honor that person.

More Ideas

Use these ideas with motivated students who want to help as individuals.

♥ Encourage your neighbors to set up a Neighborhood Watch program.

♥ Join a local chapter of an organization that protects rights and promotes justice.

♥ Learn nonviolent conflict resolution techniques and put them to work in your own life and with your friends and family.

♥ Find out if your community has a Peer Court program and volunteer.

♥ When you see examples of injustice in everyday life, speak out!

♥ Be on the lookout for suspicious behavior, watch closely from a safe distance and report your observations to the appropriate authorities.

♥ Keep learning about the issues and expressing your informed views to your local paper, local government officials and national politicians.

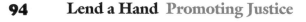

Encoded Message Puzzle

Use the code below to read the secret message about justice.

A = 26   B = 24   C = 22   D = 20   E = 18   F = 16   G = 14
H = 12   I = 10   J = 8   K = 6   L = 4   M = 2   N = 25
O = 23   P = 21   Q = 19   R = 17   S = 15   T = 13   U = 11
V = 9   W = 7   X = 5   Y = 3   Z = 1

The secret message:

J U S T I C E   M E A N S   P R O T E C T I N G
8 11 15 13 10 22 18   2 18 26 25 15   21 17 23 13 18 22 13 10 25 14

E V E R Y O N E S ,   R I G H T S   A N D
18 9 18 17 3 23 25 18 15   17 10 14 12 13 15   26 25 20

T R E A T I N G   P E O P L E   E Q U A L L Y .
13 17 18 26 13 10 25 14   21 18 23 21 4 18   18 19 11 26 4 4 3

The United Nations

Use this worksheet to help you learn about this global organization dedicated to peace, justice and equal rights for all the world's people. Use classroom, school media center and other resources to complete the worksheet.

History of the UN

• When was the United Nations established? _____

• Who was involved in starting it? _____
_____

• What was it supposed to do? _____
_____

• Name the organization that was formed after World War I to serve some of the same functions later assigned to the UN. _____

Organs and Agencies of the UN

• What are the six charter organs of the UN? _____
_____

• What are the responsibilities of each? _____
_____

• What are some of the working agencies of the UN? _____
_____

• What are the responsibilities of each? _____
_____

Successes and Failures

• What are some of the successes or accomplishments of the UN? _____
_____

• What parts of its purpose has the UN been unable to fulfill? _____
_____

Differing Opinions

• People have different opinions about how effective the UN is and can be in today's world. Based on your research, do you think the UN can succeed at building and maintaining global peace and justice? Why or why not?

_____
_____
_____
_____